From

MW00850054

"An absolute page turner, if you're ready for a glimpse into the high-stakes world of emergency services, this is the book. From beginning to end, it had me. It's so much more than 911 Dispatching, it's the heart of why some folk wake up every day and face the worst of humanity. Anhalt champion's dark humor and the compassion it takes to be a 911 Dispatcher. I couldn't put it down."

—*Miranda Levi, award winning author of*
From A Youth A Fountain Did Flow
& A Tear In Time

"Told in the honest, dry wit of someone who has been there, From the 911 Files is an eye-opening look behind the scenes at the people we depend upon to answer our emergency calls. The story within is captivating and well-written, making the audience a part of the action as we delve into what it means to be a dispatcher in today's chaotic world. Full of heart, gritty truth, and enough humor to soften the blow, I recommend this book to anyone who wants to see the reality faced by the heroes we look to in our darkest hour."

— *Cheree Alsop, author of the*
Werewolf Academy series.

FROM THE
911 Files

TRUE CRIME CONFESSIONS
FROM BEHIND THE PHONE

JACKSON ANHALT

COVER ART BY MIRANDA LEVI
IG: MIRANDALEVIAUTHOR
HTTPS://MIRANDALEVI.COM/

HTTP://JACKSONANHALT.COM
HTTPS://RQPUBLISHING.COM/

ISBN : 979-8-218-21191-2

Dedication

This book is dedicated to all who have experienced loss, tragedy, and adversity. "From the 911 Files" is a labor of love. It's themes of resilience, courage, and hope are universal and relevant to anyone who has ever faced challenges.

To the first responders who put themselves in harm's way to protect others, to the medical professionals who work tirelessly to heal the sick and injured, and to the everyday heroes who quietly make a difference in their communities, this book is dedicated to you. Your selflessness and dedication inspire us all.

To Skyler, I love you forever.

Additionally, I would like to dedicate this book to my family and friends, whose unwavering support and encouragement have been a constant source of inspiration throughout my writing career. Thank you for believing in me and constantly pushing me to be my best, especially Chris, the firefighter.

Finally, to the readers who have taken the time to explore this story, I am grateful for your willingness to engage with new ideas and perspectives. I hope that "From the 911 Files" will entertain, challenge, and inspire you and remind you of the power of human connection, empathy, and hope in the face of adversity.

The following is a re-telling of 911 events during my tenure as a 911 dispatcher. All names, dates, and locations have been changed to protect the parties' identities, even mine. All events that happen at a 911-call center are public record. Consider this an added level of precaution. Please enjoy.

Jackson Anhalt

1
An Introduction To The World Of 911

Dispatch: 911, where is your emergency?
Elderly Female Caller: Well, this really isn't an emergency.
Dispatch: Ok, well, what's going on?
Elderly Female Caller: I sat down for dinner tonight. I made soup. I called my husband to the table. We were having our dinner.
Dispatch: What exactly do you want to report?
Elderly Female Caller: Well, my husband passed out in his soup.
Dispatch: Is he breathing?
Elderly Female Caller: No.

I have a gunshot wound to the head, a shoplifter in custody at Walmart, a few traffic stops, and a guy masturbating at the park," I said, handing my headset to my partner.

"Sounds good. Have a good break. See you in fifteen minutes."

Fifteen whole minutes of freedom. I can really take the time to reflect on my morning, the pursuit that ended in a crash on the highway, the death of the elderly man at the nursing home, and the 18 traffic stops I'd completed before consuming a single sip of my coffee.

Only joking, of course. Fifteen minutes is enough to refill my water, go pee, get back to my station, and plug in so the next person can have their fifteen minutes.

At the 911 Communications Center, we are always *on*.

There's an expectation that when you lift the phone and dial those three numbers, someone will help you. We've trained entire generations to know that help is merely a call away. Unfortunately, it has become evident that the population of the United States of America has no idea what an actual emergency is.

People call 911 to report that the sheets on a hotel bed are soiled, management refuses to acknowledge their complaint, McDonald's was out of French fries, or their cat was stuck up a tree. 911 dispatchers have become a complaint line for a nation's worth of issues because, above anything else, we always answer the phone.

On the contrary, non-emergency line callers will report that their neighbor's house is fully engulfed in flames.

I can no longer count the times I've heard cries of pain and sorrow. Of mothers who have just lost their child, the shrill passion and agony from a domestic violence situation, or the last breath of a person who has just died while I sit on the other end of the line, unable to do anything but listen.

"How was your break?" Laura asked as she handed me back my headset.

"Oh, it was wonderful! I went to the coffee shop, got a latte, and chatted up that new girl. She went on and on about how excited she was to return to school. Did you know she's studying to become an esthetician?"

"Water and pee then?" she smiled.

"Yep."

"Well, you didn't miss anything. The dead guy is still dead, the Walmart thief is en route to jail, and they cleared the park;

told him to move along and find a more appropriate place to pleasure himself." Laura left, off to the next desk, to relieve another coworker.

I am a 911 Dispatcher, and this is my story.

In 2015, according to the National 911 Progress Report, 911 received 213 million calls in the United States. These calls come from landlines, cellular, VoIP lines, MLTS, and now Text-To-911. After using one of these to place your call to 911, your call is routed, based on the type of device you are using, to your designated PSAP.

Another call showed up on my screen—a barking dog complaint. I checked the location history and saw the same call type in the history field almost daily for the past two months. I looked at the Reporting Parity's (RP) name, Mr. Kenneth Jones[1]. I know this man at this point; I speak to him daily. I giggled audibly at the fact that I interacted with this man more than my best friend.

"Dispatch to Charlie-20, barking dog complaint – 11230 54th Ave to your screen," I said as I attached his number to the call on the computer.

"Charlie-20 copy," he likely sighed heavily in his patrol car, wondering what he did to upset me. One of the privileges of being me is that I decide which officer does what. Give me some sass again, Charlie-15 and your day will be littered with

---

[1] The person who calls 911 to report something, is called the RP.

barking dogs, lengthy reports, and old people wanting to explain everything that's happened to them since 1940.

It doesn't always work out that way. In this case, Charlie-20 had been my only available unit to send.

When someone calls 911 we create a ticket. These tickets are called a Call For Service or CFS. From the second we get your call processed via your location, the CFS shows in our Computer Aided Dispatch system, otherwise known as CAD. This is a system where the dispatcher and call takers can enter information, prioritize calls, and identify the status of responders who are in the field. It's the most important software we have as dispatchers. Based on pre-determined factors such as county vs. city jurisdiction or specific fire grid, the address is pre-loaded with different response types based on your need. For example, if it is a police call, it will recommend the closest unit, or the specific officer assigned to your beat for the particular shift or day. If it is a fire or aid call, it will send the closest units based on your fire grid.

I took a sip of coffee. It's cold. I know I should switch to a cold brew, but oddly, I've gotten used to cold hot coffee and prefer it to room-temperature cold brew. I looked at the clock for the 100th time in an hour. A ding goes off in my ear, bringing my attention back to the CAD for another call.

It was a 911 hang-up.

This happens several times an hour and is routine. Sometimes they are pocket dials, or "butt dials"[2] as I like to

---

[2] I'd like to have a spreadsheet one day, that will show me how many hours

call them. Sometimes they're not. The call-taker attempts to talk to whoever is there, and if they don't receive a response, they also attempt a TTY/TDD challenge. On the off chance that it is a deaf or hard-of-hearing individual is calling, they would use special telecommunications equipment to call 911. After a few more seconds with no response, they document the call's general location as given by the phone system, disconnect, and then attempt a call back the number.

For landlines, the process of a 911 hang-up is straightforward. If you call 911 from a landline, the call is traced through the phone number. Every landline phone number is attached to an exact location. 911 receives the ANI/ALI, preloaded with a name, address, phone number, etc.

Cellular calls are slightly more sophisticated. Depending on the type of cell phone you are using, the call is routed to the nearest Public Safety Answering Point, called a PSAP, based on your geographical location. The geographical location varies based on the strength of your signal and the towers your cell phone is pulling from. Larger companies' smartphones, paid lines, and cell phones will provide better locations.

Cell phones come into the CAD system at either Phase 1 or 2. Phase 1 is almost useless for ANI/ALI. It chooses the PSAP based entirely on the cellular tower the phone was last pinging off. If your phone pings off a tower in another county, across the water, or even another country, your

---

of my life I've spent listening to folk's butts.

location could be challenging to track by phone. In most cases, Phase 1 is worthless.

Phase 2 phone calls come into the CAD system, and their accuracy varies. However, we can generally pinpoint the location within a few meters. It is not, by any means, a perfect science. A 911 dispatcher is taught never to rely solely on Phase 2 hits; it is meant as a tool and a guide. Our first question will always be, "Where is your emergency?"

No answer on callback, according to the CAD screen. The call is now ready to dispatch. I debated whether I should give it to Charlie-20 again. He was clear of the barking dog complaint. I scanned the screen for anyone else who may be available. Charlie-20 has done nothing to me today and therefore deserves no punishment. Charlie-15 was also available, and although he hadn't done anything to me yet, he's done me dirty in the past, and I hold grudges.

"Dispatch to Charlie-15, 911 cellular hang-up in the area of 1502 115th Street – no answer on callback details to your screen." I imagined Charlie-20 breathing a sigh of relief that I chose another victim for what promised to be a boring call.

"Charlie-15 copy."

Sometimes I wonder whether these dramas I make up in my head about the officers are remotely based on truth. It would be easy to ask sometime in passing. I decided to keep playing it out in my head a long time ago and never know the truth. It keeps me entertained and makes the day go by faster.

"Hey, did you hear what happened with Sheila the other day?" Jon, my coworker from the next cubicle, asked between calls.

"I did not," I said.

"She was dispatching on the north radio, and we got this call about a dude who had been run over by a van. The driver was this neighbor with whom he'd been feuding for several months. An ongoing issue –David-14, I copy, I'll show you en route," Jon said.

We never get to complete a story. I've gotten so used to hearing stories in snips and clips.

"Anyway," Jon continued, "Terrance was the call-taker and saw that we've got extensive history at their address. Unfortunately, we cannot send aid directly to the scene since we have no idea where the suspect is. Also, he's known to carry guns. Sheila puts the call out ok. But she never ran the freaking suspect!"

Running a suspect is a fundamental and essential part of our job. For example, if we have an individual's name and date of birth, we can run them through the local, state, and national databases. From this, we can determine if the suspect has any outstanding warrants, if they're flagged for violent history, etc.

"Wow. I cannot believe that. Shelia is not *that* new here. I can't believe how lax the training has gotten. Back when I was in training, if I didn't run the suspect on an in-progress emergency before the officers got on scene, I would have been hit with the cattle prod," I said.

"Right?" Jon laughs. "It was especially awful this time because we started to stage the aid crew. The dude was badly injured, as you can imagine being run over by a freaking van!"

15

"Sure. Hold on," I said, then pressed the pedal beneath my desk. "Copy Charlie-15 checked the area, and nothing was found. I'll show you clear of that and send you a parking complaint at 15th near Washington Street. Blue van on the scene for several days, no plates."

"Charlie-15 copy."

The poor sap.

"Anyway, so was the guy wanted for something then?" I turn back to Jon.

"No, even better. The guy lives a mile up the street, which she would have known had she run the dude. The call taker gives care instructions to the RP, who I think was the wife or girlfriend," Jon's stories are never short.

"She is just babysitting the situation until the officers arrive on the scene. Guess where Miss Sheila stages the aid crew?" Jon pauses. "Right at the dude's house a mile away!"

"Oh shit. Did anyone get hurt?" I asked in genuine shock.

"Thankfully, no." Jon continued his rant about how Sheila received no reprimand from the supervisors and how it's so unfair because he was reprimanded for something minor in comparison.

This was a responder safety issue, and Jon felt Shelia should have been talked to. I agreed that responder safety was a matter of utmost importance.

Dispatchers are the guardians of the guardians. A dispatcher's primary function is the safety of our firefighters, paramedics, EMTs, and police officers. Our questions, however annoying they might appear, are there to provide you with the best service by getting you the most appropriate response to your needs. It's also to protect the people we have coming to help you.

It's vital that we know if weapons are on scene or accessible so we do not send unarmed fire and aid personnel into an unsafe situation. In addition, we need to know about drug and or alcohol usage because people under the influence respond differently than those who are not. A firefighter, paramedic, EMT, or an officer's primary job function is to protect and serve their community. Your tax dollars fund them and are there for you.

"Dispatch to Charlie-20 – 911 VoIP line – 2323 Monroe Street, brief open line with what sounded like a child playing on the phone, no answer on callback," I said.

"Charlie-20, show me en route."

VoIP and MTLS lines are only as good as the person who owns them. If you have one of these phone lines, please ensure your home or business address and information are always accurate with the company.

There are endless stories of 911 calls from these types of phones. Only the addresses we received were with the ANI/ALI from the VoIP line. This would be okay if the information were kept up to date, but it often isn't. The RPs move, and no, they can't speak freely on the phone, or the call is disconnected before the dispatcher can confirm an address. 911 calls are often made under the most horrific circumstances.

One such example happened a few years ago. A colleague of mine received a call from a domestic violence victim. She got all the correct information; victim name, suspect name, weapon description, vehicle description, etc. The police arrived at the address in the call, and no one was home. The dispatcher had gotten all the information but did not confirm the address. She relied solely on the ANI/ALI from the VoIP line. The subjects moved a few months before the event and still need to update their address with their phone provider. They were not even in the same state. These phones are *programmed* to dial 911. They will dial the closest PSAP based on the pre-programmed address, not their physical location. Thankfully, the dispatcher was able to reconnect with the victim in time to connect her with her local 911 Communications Center–it ended well. Unfortunately, we aren't always so lucky.

"Charlie-20 on scene."

"Copy on scene." I change his status in CAD. As dispatchers, we always think ahead of the officer—ever ready for all outcomes. In this case, I put him on scene. I am now anticipating several potential developments from him.

The most likely will be, "Show me clear, false alarm, a child playing with a phone." That made the most sense in this particular case. However, my job is always to play the *what-if* game.

What if, this time, it was a child trying to call 911 because his parents were fighting? They noticed and then took the phone away. If the officer just accepted this call as a kid playing with a phone and failed to go and check it out, there could be potential for all sorts of disasters. Someone called for help, and the officer went.

"Charlie-20, send me an additional unit. We have a domestic violence situation," *could* very well have been his following sentence. "Charlie-20, send an ambulance. We've got an injured male, 20s, fell in a bathtub," or "Charlie-20, I have an open door, give me the air, secure the tones, I am going to check the residence." I am giving a quick scan to units nearby, ensuring I have the call ready for dispatch for aid if needed. The potential for something to go horribly wrong exists on every single call. I must be ever diligent and prepared for anything.

"Charlie-20, show me clear, false alarm, a child playing with phone."

Figures.

You could say I have a flair for the dramatic. I believe a proclivity for drama, a dark sense of humor, skin as thick as dragon scales, a highly organized demeanor with a hint of obsessive compulsiveness, and an insatiable desire to be needed are the requirements of a great dispatcher. No machine can compare to the efficiency of a 911 dispatch center coming together over a major incident. For better or worse, we are all addicted to the rush. It's our heroin. Three-vehicle rollover collision with seven injured? Yeah, baby, give it to me!

The clock says I've been here for 4 hours. I was in disbelief. Surely, I had been here for at least twelve hours already. My stomach grumbled. I thought of my lunch break, which was still another hour away. I reached down into my snack pack (backpack) for something to tide me over.

My snack pack has become something of a legend in the dispatch center. Everyone knew I always carried goodies around. Feeling low on energy, ask Jackson! He's got a nice pick-me-up—a granola bar for Gretchen, an apple for Annie, and a juice box for Jon. The snack pack was not limited to just food either. I always had a healthy stock of tissues, aspirin, antacids, band-aids, and an assortment of pens, markers, and other office supplies. Unfortunately, 911 Dispatch Centers are rarely stocked adequately for the needs of their employees. We, being resourceful people, take care of not only the community we serve but also each other.

Carrie, our mother figure and twenty-five-year dispatch veteran, also carries a stockpile of everything you could ever need or want. She moved her stuff around in a piece of wheeled luggage, the carry-on size. Watching her leave work was always comical. One of the newbie dispatchers asked if she was leaving for a vacation the first time, she saw her clock off from work. Admittedly, it looked like she was ever ready for a Vegas vacation. I laughed and advised her to ask Carrie directly. Knowing full-well how many times she'd been asked that questions before.

A few more routine calls came in, and I dispatched them out––a phone call request about a civil dispute between a neighbor's property line, a three-car pile-up, and a text-to-911 report of suspicious activity.

Text-to-911 is still an extremely new edition to the 911 accessibility tool bag. It's also the worst at getting location. ANI/ALI cannot re-establish a connection the way it can with a cellular call. The confidence reading of Text-to-911 is similar to a Phase 1 cellular hit.

Text-to-911 is recommended when a call to 911 is impossible due to the inability to speak freely or otherwise. It is also an excellent tool for the deaf and hard of hearing; TTY software still exists and is available at all 911 PSAPs nationwide. Please still call 911 if you are able. We get the best information in a timelier manner from a phone call.

Finally, it was time for lunch.

More accurately, my thirty-minute break where I, once again, fill my water, pee, and cram down whatever crap I brought to be reheated in the nasty work microwave that hasn't been cleaned since the 1970s. Thirty minutes is not enough time to go anywhere and buy something fresh.

Back to the confinement of my desk. I glanced at the clock. Only three more hours until I can go home. I quickly scan my calls to see what I've missed during my lunch break—nothing interesting. Double checked my roster, and off I went.

"What are you going to do with your days off?" Laura's voice comes from Jon's cubical. He must be off to lunch.

"Nothing special. Just get some stuff done around the house and spend time with my kiddo. You?" I don't really care, but the chit-chat fills the void.

"Days off? What are those?" Laura poked back.

"Ha. Working your days off again? By choice?" I asked, slightly worried about my days off.

"Nope. I got mandatory overtime on my Saturday."

"That sucks. I'm sorry. I got called in on my Sunday last week because there was no one to cover," I told her with actual empathy.

The dispatch center needs to be staffed at a minimal level 24 hours a day, seven days a week, 365 days a year. Crime does not take a break, and neither do we. Every dispatch center works a schedule to cover its needs. Sometimes that schedule is kind to employees, but more often, it's not. At my center, we work a *week* and have *weekends*, but they aren't on a typical Monday through Friday schedule. Instead of it being Wednesday, the 22nd of August, today is *my* Friday. Thursday and Friday are *my* Saturday and Sunday, respectively.

Fear not. It confuses my family and close friends as well.

Our days off rotate so that in a perfect world, if there were no sick call-ins and vacations to cover, we each share in working part of the weekends so that once or twice a month, we can have them off— true Saturday and Sundays. It is a feeble attempt to live an everyday life and see our family and friends with regular schedules.

At least another half of an hour has passed as I am getting more and more excited to go home. I start thinking about all the everyday activities I have to do. Make dinner, vacuum the living room, and put away the laundry that's been in the dryer the past two days.

I dispatched another routine call to Charlie-15 when I spotted her out of the corner of my eye.

It's the supervisor, Audrey, and she was coming my way.

"Hey, Jackson," she said.

"I hate you. Go away!" I whined. I know what's coming.

"I'm sorry, you know I hate doing this as much as you hate being told," I believed her. It can't be fun to be in her position, either. You know the old expression *Don't kill the messenger?* In this case, the messenger is all I have, and something has to die!

"You're a mean-spirited person, and I hope you trip on the way back to your desk," she's used to my antics.

"We had a sick call in, and I must mandate you to stay."

I knew this was coming. It happens all the time. However, I take every opportunity to act like an overgrown toddler. I flopped onto my desk and bowled over in fake tears.

"Sorry, dude."

She walked away, and I returned to my usual professional self, whining to no less than three other coworkers about it. If I had to be the unlucky one today, everyone would know about it.

My household duties could and would have to wait another day because, after a twelve-hour shift, particularly one that was not pre-planned, all I can do is pour myself into bed when I get home. So far, my weekend was still safe. I looked over at Audrey, who was back at her desk on the phone with someone from two shifts from now, telling them they'd need to come in early to cover the 2nd half of the next shift and relieve me. Oh well, such is life in this crazy profession I have chosen.

I am thrilled to report that I am never bored with my job. Despite feeling like I have heard it all, it's always interesting. This career has taken so much from me; my time, energy, social life, and even to a certain degree, my soul. The benefits are alright. At my center, we are lucky enough to have decent health insurance, which in today's America, is worth its weight in gold. We still have a decent retirement package with a 401k-type matching program and a state-paid pension. However, the pay is severely lacking across the board, and we are still not counted as "first responders" in the United States. We are still considered "secretarial workers" and not to undermine the responsibilities of secretaries everywhere, but when have they ever had to sit and listen to someone die, unable to do anything?

So, why do I do it?

Nothing else fulfills me like this career.

When I talk a call from a screaming mother whose baby has stopped breathing—I am able to calm her down and give her infant CPR instructions while simultaneously dispatching police and aid to her location. Together, because of my efforts, by the time I hang up the phone and the help arrives, I hear the cries of the toddler coming back to life. No words can describe that feeling.

I made a difference.

I saved a life.

2

I'll Have A Murder, Please, With A Side Of Nachos.

Dispatch: 911, where is your emergency?

Male Caller: Off of Lake Rd and Bonny Hill Rd.

Dispatch: Ok, well, what's going on?

Male Caller: There's an abandoned vehicle here off to the side of the roadway. It's a blue Honda Civic, license plate ABC123.

Dispatch: Ok, is it blocking the roadway at all?

Male Caller: No, it's pulled off the side and... oh, I think someone's sleeping in it.

Dispatch: Ok, are they breathing?

Male Caller: Yeah, I think so, it's a woman, and she's sleeping on the steering wheel.

Dispatch: Ok, are you able to see if you can wake her?

Male Caller: Sure, uhm.... Wait.... I don't think she's breathing.

Dispatch: Oh? What do you see?

Male Caller: Nope.... Oh god.... Nope... she is definitely... no.... she is not breathing.

Dispatch: Ok, can you get her out of the vehicle and start CPR?

Male Caller: Maybe? There's so much blood.

Dispatch: Ok, do you see any obvious wounds anywhere?

Male Caller: Ahhhh! Yeah.... Uhm... yeah...

Dispatch: What?

Male Caller: *choking* She has a gunshot wound to the head. She's dead. Half of her head is blown off.

Dispatch: Do you see the gun anywhere?

Male Caller: Yes, it's right next to her.

Dispatch: Ok, why don't you step away from the car, and we'll take it from here? Thank you for attempting to assist.

April 21ST, 2014 – 12 Hour Shift

Early in the morning, nearing the end of our shift, my coworker Jon and I were talking about how quiet the night was—a grave mistake. The golden rule in dispatch is never to say the word *quiet* in the communications center.

Saying *quiet* is as cursed as saying *MacBeth* backstage in a theatre.

The exact moment the Q–word was uttered, the phone rang.

I answered.

The RP was the mother of a suicidal individual. What started as a reasonably routine suicide call quickly took a turn for the weird.

The RP's son shot himself in the head.

While I was attempting to find out the location of the body and updating the units en route to the call, the RP told me her son had just jumped out of a 2nd story window.

As you can imagine, Jon and I were confused. How does a person who just shot himself in the head jump out of a window?

I clarified with the caller her son just, in fact, shot himself in the head.

Yes.

And then he jumped out the window?

Yes.

The RP told me her son was on the back lawn attempting to slit his wrists with a knife.

Are you keeping up?

After updating the police units en route to the call, the RP told me her husband was able to get the knife away from her son. However, the suspect was still on the lawn, bleeding out.

"Uhm, there's a lot about this call I don't understand, dude," Jon said as he got the aid crew en route.

"Same," I said.

"So, did he actually shoot himself in the head?" Jon asked.

"That's what she said. I confirmed it with her twice," I said.

Sometimes when there's a lack of good information, dispatchers can turn on each other and blame the call-taker for not getting the information correctly. But, in truth, we all know we are only as good as the people providing the information.

When law enforcement arrived on the scene, they made contact with the son in the backyard. He was semi-compliant with the officer.

This suicide call took a turn when the son became a suspect. He started babbling incoherently about how he "had to kill her because she was a spy."

Unsure of what the suspect was saying, being the only officer on the scene and given the gunshot wound and self-harm with a knife, the officer waited for another unit before sweeping through the house and property.

Over the radio, I heard one last sentence that still haunts me: "Dispatch, we have a 2nd victim, a female…black."

We don't have codes anymore in dispatch. Before my time, they used a lot of 10-codes.

Most people have heard of a 10-code, although you might not know what it means off the top of your head. Ten-code is officially called ten signals. Essentially, they are brevity codes used to represent a list of common phrases when speaking on the radio. "10-4" for example, means "Copy" or "I understand". 10-60 refers to a responder's private residence. And at one point in time, 10-99 meant wanted or stolen. There was a whole list of 10-codes, averaging 100 to a department, each dispatcher would have to memorize.

After September 11, 2001, when two planes struck the Twin Towers in New York City[1], law enforcement agencies everywhere had to abandon 10-code. 9/11 was a large-scale disaster. Responding units came from agencies located all over the greater New York City area. However, each of their "codes" meant different things.

There was never uniform coding, therefore, they had an extremely difficult time communicating over the radio. 10-6 might mean "all clear" to one agency and "man down" in another. Mass chaos ensued when all those units started sharing a single incident command frequency.

---

[1] Maybe you've heard of it?

To smooth over this process, the government mandated all responses would follow a simplified and unified "Incident Command" wherein plain English was used, and certain titles and responsibilities would be unified. The federal government decided, for any agency to receive federal funding, they would comply with new regulations. After this, multi-agencies responses have become a lot smoother, not to mention safer.

There are still some simple codes in existence. For example, when getting on any scene, patients can be classified in one of four ways: Green, Yellow, Red, or Black. Green patients are okay, possible cuts and bruises, but fine without immediate care. Yellow patients require care, however, their status is not immediately life-threatening. Red patients need immediate attention, or they are likely to die quickly. Lastly, Black patients are bereft of life.

The story of suicide and murder unfolded. The killer was the RP's son. He suffered a life-long struggle with mental health problems. These mental health concerns were exacerbated by methamphetamine abuse. The female victim, of the suicidal killer was strangled. She was his twenty-year-old girlfriend. The murder felt guilty about his actions and attempted to kill himself.

Three times.

Later, the suspect would plead guilty in court before it went to trial and receive up to 18 years in prison. I don't always have the ability to follow up on my calls, but for my first murder, I needed to know how it ended.

"Well, that was an interesting way to end the shift," Jon said, finally breaking the silence. The initial excitement of the event calmed down. "I do believe you have earned your first nachos."

"Nachos?" I asked.

"Nachos," Megan said as she walked into the room to relieve me, with Pam behind her. "Uh oh, Jackson, who did you kill? At least tell me you guys cleaned it before we take over."

"Oh, yeah, it's all pretty much wrapped up," Jon explained the event, the information we had, and how it all ended up being outrageously true.

"Damn! You earned those nachos!" Pam said.

"Is someone going to explain this nacho thing to me?" I asked.

"Whenever you have a death on your shift, and you're the call-taker, you get nachos," said Megan. "How have you been here almost two years and not heard of nachos yet?"

"This is my first murder," I explained.

"It doesn't have to be a murder to count. I got nachos a couple of weeks ago for a CPR call. The poor guy had been dead at least overnight. We attempted CPR anyway. It didn't work," said Jason.

The group went on to tell various stories about their most recent nacho acquisitions.

According to Pam, nachos started many years before I ever considered working in dispatch. Allegedly, it began as a misheard statement. The sergeant on duty came into the dispatch center and noticed a newer dispatcher was feeling down about a death she had recently dispatched. The sergeant told her it would be "just a notch in your belt" after a while... but somehow, someone misheard his comment as "nachos." Thus, nachos after death was born.

After the conversation with my coworkers, I learned there are specific rules about transference that are highly debated among the dispatchers. For instance, if you took a call about someone who fell down the stairs, but they don't die till the next day, does that still count as a nachos?

The very next shift, Jon bought me nachos.

A 20-year-old girl was murdered. There was nothing we could do for her.

Jon disagreed. He said we were there for the survivors and did what we could to bring her murderer to justice.

I thought about how morbid it was that we were celebrating death by eating nachos. Jon reminded me that part of our job is dealing with horrendous situations, and we must take care of ourselves. Somehow, weirdly, I earned those nachos.

They were delicious.

August 18TH, 2014 – 8 Hour Shift

My second murder was just a few months after the first. The call came early into my shift. I had been there for barely an hour.

The RP was a passerby who found a body on the side of the road. The victim appeared to have been riding her bike before being struck by a car and left for dead. Based on the caller's descriptions, it was not immediately clear whether or not the victim was alive.

After law enforcement arrived, someone attempted CPR, and the victim was pronounced dead at the scene. Now, the trick was to figure out who hit her.

"You know, on that rural highway, there's going to be a slim chance of any witnesses," Jon said.

The deputy on the case found some fragments of the suspect vehicle. Based on the pieces he gathered, the deputy believed the suspect's vehicle to be a pickup truck, black in color, and headed out of town. The truck would have significant front end and passenger side wheel well damage. I notified the other agencies in the area to watch for such a vehicle.

After the aid crew and law enforcement were on scene for 30 minutes, completing their investigations, we received another 911 call relating to this case. The female RP stated her estranged husband showed up at her house randomly. He told the RP he thinks he killed a woman. He was scared and went to her. He was afraid to turn himself in. The RP listened to the scanner and heard her husband's victim did not survive. At this point, she called 911 and insisted he turns himself in.

After providing answers to the dispatcher, the RP hung up and drove her husband to the crime scene. Within a few minutes, an officer took him into custody. Deputies followed the RP to her home and secured the suspect vehicle—a black truck with front-end damage.

"It makes me feel good when a plan comes together," I said triumphantly, as if I had solved this crime. The phone rang again. It was the on-scene deputy.

Jon took the call after explaining what the deputy said. "As it turns out, the suspect, presumably under the influence of methamphetamines, was driving southbound on the highway. He hit the victim, pulled over a few hundred yards ahead, turned around, and drove northbound into town."

"Damn," I said.

"The dude actually slowed down to see he hit the woman with his truck and then continued in the opposite direction towards his estranged wife's house."

"Jesus," I said. "The victim might have lived if he'd just stopped and called 911. Do we know who the victim was?"

"The victim was Amber Jermain," Jon said.

Amber was a known methamphetamine addict in the area. She had been a problem for the local law enforcement for years. Amber would call 911 four or five days a week to report her bicycle stolen. Only she never wanted to file an official report. Instead, Amber wanted the officers to come out and help her look for it—preferably a young, tall, dark, and handsome officer.

She made special requests.

Amber's anecdotes started small. After the bicycle trick stopped working, her frequent 911 calls became more elaborate. Finally, she worked up to a false rape report.

Typically, I suggest believing anyone who reports sexual assault. But this was quite the story.

A white male in his 40s drove up in a yellow sports car and grabbed her right off the street. He told Amber that he was a Wall Street executive in town on business worth hundreds of billions of dollars. This Wall Street savant offered her the lead role in a Hollywood movie. He apparently had all kinds of connections. He offered Amber all of this in exchange for sex. Amber claims she said no, and when he wouldn't let her out, she kicked and screamed in the front seat, unable to escape. From there, he drove her to a secluded area and had his way with her. Then he left to catch a red-eye plane back to New York City.

Despite having no evidence, many holes in the timeline of her story, and extremely vague suspect descriptions, the officers did their due diligence. They investigated as if it were an actual crime. Amber was transported to the emergency room, where she was examined with a rape kit. She showed no signs of sexual contact, no symptoms of a struggle, marks, scratches, or bruises. She divulged to the on-scene nurse that she made up the entire story because she wanted to see if Officer Sanders was working. She was eventually charged with false reporting.

Amber would get herself into real trouble from time to time. Ironically, these would go largely unreported. An officer told me about a year before she was murdered, he found Amber beaten, bloody, and near a dumpster behind a grocery store. She refused to answer any questions about her situation. Amber also refused aid. Unable to prove any crime, the officer asked her to move along from behind the grocery store. Officers spoke with other known cohorts of Ambers. They were able to ascertain she allegedly owed money to her dealer. She'd been beaten when she couldn't pay.

No one would come forward and write a witness statement on Amber's behalf. She refused to be a victim. There is no crime without a willing victim. A year later, someone killed her.

It is unknown if Amber and the suspect who hit her with his truck knew each other.

Was this just an unfortunate coincidence? Was Amber simply riding her bike at the wrong place or time? Or was this a more complicated drug deal gone bad?

I don't know.

Proving this was an intentional act of murder would be a tough sell to any jury. The suspect pleaded guilty while in jail and was sentenced to ten years in prison for vehicular homicide.

The rest of the shift was a blur. The incident took up much of the deputies' resources and time. When officers are on a call like this, it prevents them from being proactive.[2]

"You know, we're starting to become quite the crime-fighting pair," I said.

Jon chuckled, "Yeah, too bad it's slowed down."

"That's the downside of a major incident early on in your shift," I said.

---

[2] And by proactive, I mean drive through areas of high crime, drive by homes listed on the 'request to watch' list, and run by the convivence store to grab me an energy drink.

"More time for reflection and self-awareness," Jon said.

"Yeah? Do you think about this horrible incident and how we were once again able to be there for the recently departed? Not to mention being able to bring her murderer to justice. Are we supposed to have some moment of self-love?" I asked.

"God no, nothing like that," he chuckled. "I was just wondering whether to get chicken or beef for your nachos tomorrow."

"Oh! Chicken, please."[3]

"You know who really hated Amber?" Jon said.

"No."

"Our coworker Pam. She had so many bad run-ins with her over the years. One time, she called in and really had her going. She reported that someone was actively trying to kidnap her. Apparently, it sounded convincing. There was a physical altercation. She was out of breath, screaming on the other end. Pam sent the police on high alert. She even got aid and fire out, looking for the truck involved in the kidnapping," Jon laughed hard, "She processed the entire call and only got the name at the end. It was Amber."

"So it was all a lie?" I asked.

"Yep. Every bit of it."

I laughed at Pam's misfortune, but the truth is that we all fall victim to believing the lies that people call 911 to report. The police are also very understanding with us when this happens. Unfortunately, even though we do our best to filter this type of RP, everyone gets bamboozled now and again.

---

[3] Sidenote, no one asked for, that chicken gave me food poisoning. I was on the toilet for half my shift.

"Good morning," Jon said to someone over my shoulder.

"Good evening to you," Pam said. She and Megan were coming in to relieve us.

"You're never going to believe who Jackson killed last night," Jon said. "Amber!"

Pam's smile beamed across the room, a rare sight indeed. Especially so early in the morning. "I need to get you something nice."

January 18TH, 2017 – 12 Hour Shift

We have shots fired, and I need an ambulance here immediately!" The call started with a suspicious male inside a thrift store. The man was "dancing" erratically, slurring his words and talking about the government. Specifically, he spoke about how they planted chips inside his brain to control his mind.

When the man wouldn't leave, the thrift store employee understandably called 911. The first officer got on the scene rather quickly. He called for a backing officer, routine. After a few minutes, two additional officers got on the scene.

The unwelcome man continued his rant about the government and how ISIS would capture his consciousness and make him do bad things.

The officers employed many techniques to placate the man. First, they talked to him calmly and softly to get him to listen. Then, they stepped into his world and tried to rationalize with him on his level by asking about the chips in his head. They offered to take him to the hospital and have them look at the chips.

Nothing worked.

The man got more and more agitated. Eventually, he ran into the middle of the highway. He crouched down in the divider and shuffled through his backpack.

He pulled out an eight-inch bladed knife, then charged at the officers.

I could write an entire novel about the political side of officer-involved shootings. This is a highly polarized topic in the media.

Instead, I'll say simply that I was not there.

I do not have all of the facts.

I will never know.

I wanted to know, so I asked what exactly was going through the officer's heads before they shot the man? He was charging at them with a weapon. And they shot him.

But answers are never so simple, especially in this situation.

All I know is my perspective.

Twenty seconds after, I heard the screams of "shots fired," tones and alarms for ambulances went out. It was an additional twenty seconds for me to mentally process what had just happened.

A man was just killed.

My officer, colleague, and friend just killed someone.

Five seconds have passed since that thought began. Only now I have to breathe and reset because the 911 line rings again...

"911, what's the address of your emergency?"

April 17TH, 2016 – 12 Hour Shift

The 911 line rang, and I answered the call.

Only this time, it seemed no one was there. I could hear breathing on the other line, but no one answered any of my questions. I chalked it up to a pocket dial, as they are ubiquitous.

When I called back, a woman answered.

The woman on the line was talking strangely. She kept referring to me as Becky. I'm not a Becky, even if I tried. My voice is deep, rough even. It was at this moment that I realized this caller was trapped.

"Are you able to speak freely?" I asked.

"No. Becky, I'm not able to go out tonight," she said.

"Alright, I understand. Are you injured?"

"No, I can't go out tomorrow night either," her voice faltered.

"Your cell phone confidence came in low. Are you by chance in Newville?" a common occurrence with this particular cell tower.

After a series of questions she could safely answer with yes or no, I determined this woman was outside my jurisdiction. I transferred her to the correct 911 agency and stayed on to provide all of the pertinent information to the new 911 dispatcher.

Later on in my shift, the other call center rang me back. They let me know the RP had a gun to her head. They appreciated my diligence with her call. It just reiterated to me: every call has the potential to be something huge. The possibility to save a life or the potential to lose one. It's a hard lesson to remember when every 911 call center receives hundreds of "butt-dials" every single day. We have to do our due diligence on each of these calls because all it takes is one person to be in trouble.

"She probably had it coming," Jon said. "I've never heard of anyone having a gun to their head that didn't have it coming."

"What about in the case of bank robberies where the one with the gun in their face is just an employee of the bank?" I asked.

"It's their fault for working at the bank."

I laughed. "What about the innocent people there just to make a deposit or take out a home loan? Are we all supposed to avoid banks because of the potential for us to have a gun in our face?"

"Yep." Jon could tell he'd been defeated in his argument. I don't think he was being serious anyway. He rarely is—one of my favorite things about him.

"Where's your compassion Jon?" a voice came from behind us.

"I lost my compassion the day I started working with you, Audrey."

The supervisor, obviously used to Jon's antics as much as anyone else's, just sighed. "That was a long time ago, my dear."

"Hey! It's not all negative," Jon said, "I've really started looking forward to death now."

July 31st, 2011 – 8 Hour Shift

Good morning, trainees. Today we're going to take a break from the console and listen to a few recordings of previous calls," my training supervisor, Audrey, said. "There are some lessons that are imperative to learn. Some of these calls are executed well. Some are not. We'll listen to these and have a short discussion afterward. Feel free to leave the room if you feel it's too much. But you should probably find a new job then as well."

Most dispatchers listen to a lot of recordings while they're in training. The very first call Audrey played for us was a difficult lesson on the importance of getting the location of the emergency first. Those in the field famously know this as the "Ruth Price" call.

Ruth was an older woman in a medium-sized city. She called the operator instead of dialing 911. The operator directly transferred her to 911. Ruth was frightened because she heard strange noises outside her apartment and wanted to report it to law enforcement. Ruth started the conversation by providing her address. Unfortunately, the dispatcher cut her off to ask what she was reporting, never getting Ruth's full address. The call continued with Ruth describing what she heard to the 911 call-taker. Not even sixty seconds pass from when Ruth is connected to 911 to when Ruth pauses to listen as someone busts through her door.

The only thing you can hear is Ruth screaming.

It sounded like she was being murdered while help was on the line, unable to do anything. The dispatcher was forced to listen to the entire attack.

The dispatcher is helpless. She cut Ruth off instead of taking her address down first. This call is available on YouTube. You can listen to it yourself if you dare.

"I didn't personally take this call, but it has always struck a chord with me," said Audrey.

We were all shell-shocked over what we had just heard.

"It reminds us always, no matter how frantic the caller is on the line, always, always, always get the location first. Then, if the line goes dead, if someone attacks the caller, if you understand nothing more, law enforcement can be sent to their location at a bare minimum. It could save a life."

"What happened to her?" one of the newbies asked.

"I'm not 100% sure, but the rumor is that she was murdered, and the police did not find her body for over a week, but I don't know officially," Audrey said.

The call became a legend for over twenty years. Recently, a few sleuths on social media were seeking answers to this old call. As I understand it, they discovered she was not, in fact, murdered. However, Ruth was severely beaten by a man attempting to burgle her residence. I have not personally verified this. If you end up researching this, let me know.

Three of us sat in the training room. We could barely look at each other. Perhaps she started with the worst call. Surely it couldn't get worse from there. Right?

I was wrong.

Audrey pushed play on the next recording.

Sometimes the best lessons are those we can learn from other people.

This call shook me to my core. While I type this, I'm getting chills just recalling the recording.

"911, where is your emergency?" the dispatcher said.

"Mommy killed us." The caller was a child.

"This is 911. Do you have an emergency?"

"Mommy killed us."

"You said your mother killed you?" disbelief evident in the dispatcher's voice.

"Mommy killed us."

"This is 911. Where's your mom? Let me speak to her."

"Mommy killed us," the boy's voice breaks.

Another dispatcher came on the line to try to reason with the caller.

"Honey, if she killed you, how are you talking to me?" the new dispatcher said.

The RP was a 9-year-old boy. He called 911 after his mother drove him and his younger brother to a remote location. He said he was lost, and his mom was asleep in the front seat.

The 911 dispatcher asked the boy to wake his mother up. She wanted to talk to the mom to sort out what was happening. The boy said he was afraid to wake her up because she would be mad and shoot them again.

Shoot them? Did she hear him wrong?

No, she hadn't.

Earlier in the day, the RP's mother quarreled with the father of her children. After the disagreement, she loaded her two children into her Suburban. She drove aimlessly for forty-five minutes until she eventually pulled off the main roads and parked on an abandoned forest road. She threw the keys out the window. The mother pulled a gun from the glove compartment and shot both sons in the backseat before turning the gun on herself.

"Where are you?" the dispatcher asked.

"I don't know," he whimpered.

"What do you see around you?"

"Trees."

"Is there anything else? A building? A river? Anything?" You could hear the desperation in the dispatcher's voice.

This call came in at a time before 911 centers could ping the cell phone's location, and she was helpless to find the boy without his assistance.

"No. There's nothing."

"Do you remember driving by anything you recognized?"

Jackpot.

The boy described driving by a known bank in town and a grocery store. The boy then remembered seeing an uncrewed fire station. Finally, he described a truck sitting in the parking lot of a fire station.

"Where did your mother say you were going?"

"To hell."

I looked around the room in the training class. Everyone was bawling.

A lump developed in my throat, and a sinking in my stomach. The call lasted for more than forty minutes. We listened to every single second of the recording.

The dispatcher convinced the boy to crawl over his dead mother so he could turn on the vehicle's hazard lights. At one point, his phone starts to die, and she walks him through, plugging it into the car charger. The boy was terrified his mom would walk up and shoot him again. Meanwhile, his brother was unmoving, bleeding out in the seat next to his.

The dispatcher got a few more minor details out of the boy. Then, finally, she was able to narrow down the search efforts to a five-mile radius. The boy's memory of the truck in the unmanned fire station was the tip-off. A different dispatcher called around looking for anyone who owned a specific make and model truck, and they found it.

It took three police agencies and two fire agencies to locate the boy. The mother was found, as reported, in the front seat with a gunshot wound to the head. The boy's brother was pronounced dead at the scene.

"He was shot in the lung. The paramedic on the scene said he'd have died if more than a couple more minutes had passed. He was already foaming at the mouth when they arrived. But he lived. He's still alive to this day," Audrey said. "He eventually got to meet his dispatcher. He and his father wanted to thank them in person for saving the boy's life. After that, the boy visited the dispatch center about once a year until college. We must remember to use our training and resources to save lives. Any seemingly insignificant call has the potential to be something major. It is up to us as dispatchers to try to rule out the nothing calls from the ones who need our help."

Melinda, one of my fellow trainees, raised her hand. Her face was pale, obviously in shock over the call.

"Yes," Audrey pointed to Melinda, "do you have a question?"

"Is this something we can expect from this job?" Melinda said.

"Well, I mean, this does not happen every single day. This call happened almost 15 years ago. I don't, in memory, recall anything quite as morose happening since. Of course, our technology has improved significantly, and finding people has become easier. But, yes. To answer your question more honestly, you must be ready for anything. We never know what is coming in when we pick up that phone."

"I don't think I can do this," Melinda said.

We broke for lunch. Laura, the other trainee, and I spent our thirty-minute mental pause in the breakroom eating in silence.

There wasn't much to say to one another.

Melinda was absent from the breakroom. She was a smoker, so we assumed she would be out back on the patio having a cigarette or two after hearing these calls. I almost needed a cigarette myself, and I'm not a smoker.

After returning to the classroom, Audrey informed us that Melinda went to the director's office immediately after the recordings and quit.

This job is not for everyone.

November 24TH, 2016 – 12 Hour Shift

It was Thanksgiving, and we had a reported a Dead On Arrival also known as a DOA. The RP stated that the father of the family had passed away. Laura took the call, processed it, and sent the appropriate response.

"What happens now?" Laura asked the room.

"The officer gets on the scene, says 'yup, he dead.' We send the medics, and they go, 'Yup, he dead.' They request the coroner, and he says, 'Yup, y'all were right, he dead,'" Jon has an almost poetic way of explaining things.

"No, I mean, do I still get nachos?" Laura asked. "I mean, we don't really know *when* he died."

"That is an excellent point. I guess we'll have to wait and see what the officer says about the time frame. I think if they came for a visit and he's been dead for several days or more, that doesn't count because he didn't die on your shift," I explained. The rules were, after all, heavily debated.

"I didn't know it mattered so much," Jon piped in. "I mean, she did take the call, there is a body, and it happened today." Jon ticked the points off on his fingers. "I think it counts."

"I agree," Laura chimed in.

"Of course, you would agree. You're the beneficiary," I said. "If we had nachos for every single death we took, then we'd have to count the DOAs at the nursing homes too. I feel like we shouldn't count expected deaths."

The officer dispatched to the call was confused when he arrived at the house and found a happy and upbeat family. They were in the midst of making Thanksgiving dinner. The officer asked one of the family members about the deceased person. He was led upstairs to the bedroom where the body was. The family member explained to the officer how the father had eaten applesauce and passed away.

Confused, the officer started to query the household. Why had no one attempted CPR to revive the patient? The family explained that the father put drugs in his applesauce.

This was now a suicide.

Further confused, the officer was getting uneasy. Didn't they try to talk their father out of suicide? This family's complacency about the death was mind-boggling.

After more interviews, the officer began to slowly understand what happened. The random suicide was a prescription-based planned suicide. A medical professional oversaw the assisted suicide. Unfortunately, the RP, the family members on the scene, and even the medical professional all failed to mention such an important detail.

"He was diagnosed with terminal brain cancer. It was going to kill him in a horribly painful way. Instead, he chose assisted suicide as a dignified, painless alternative," explained the officer over the phone with dispatch.

"Thank you," Laura said, hanging up the phone. She turned to the rest of us. "Technically, he did die today."

"I think it counts, based on the strangeness of the entire call alone," Jon said.

"Congratulations Laura," I said. "Beef or chicken?"

We found the humor through our unique perspective and ate some tasty nachos. There was a good chuckle at the officer's unfortunate misunderstanding and a funny story to tell the grandkids.

3
Ma'am, If You Want Service, You'll Need To Put Your Pants On

Dispatch: 911, where is your emergency?

Male Caller: Down by the log dump.

Dispatch: Ok, and what is going on down at the log dump?

Male Caller: This occurred there earlier in the day. A bunch of people beat a black man. I think this was probably a hate crime.

Dispatch: To confirm, this is not in progress.

Male Caller: No, sir. This happened, I believe, earlier in the day. My friend was beaten by two other males, white males who drove up in a pickup truck, said racial slurs, and then beat the hell out of him.

Dispatch: Do you know these subjects?

Male Caller: No, sir. I don't have a clue who they were.

Dispatch: Ok, is your friend injured?

Male Caller: You bet he is. Two men beat him, what do you think?

Dispatch: Ok, does he need an ambulance?

Male Caller: Yeah, probably.

Dispatch: What is the address of his location so I can send an ambulance to him?

Male Caller: I can't tell you that! All I can tell you is that he's in a secure location only I know. Trust me; he's safe.

Dispatch: But you told me he needs an ambulance. As a friend, you should be giving him the care he needs.

Male Caller: I am! That's why I'm calling you. To let you know of this horrible crime.

Dispatch: Right, and you said he's badly injured. You said he needs an ambulance, correct?

Male Caller: Yes.

Dispatch: How can I get an ambulance to him if you don't tell me where he is?

Male Caller: You do not understand me!

Dispatch: Clearly, I do not. Can you explain again?

Male Caller: My friend, who's black, was beaten by two white men who were in a pickup truck, and they took off. He needs help.

Dispatch: Ok, I understand that. How can I help him?

Male Caller: By taking care of the situation!

Dispatch: And how can I do that?

Male Caller: You need to be taking this information! Are you even writing this down?

Dispatch: Ok, let's focus on the assailants. You said they were white men in a pickup truck, yes?

Male Caller: Yes.

Dispatch: Did you get a plate number on the pickup truck?

Male Caller: Nope.

Dispatch: Ok, what kind of truck was it?

Male Caller: I don't know.

Dispatch: Ok, what did the two guys look like, other than white men?

Male Caller: I'm not sure; why aren't you doing anything about this?

Dispatch: I am trying. So far, I've gotten two white males to beat up a black male. The black male is injured but is hidden in a secure facility, and you will not release the secured

52

location to me. The suspects were driving a pickup truck of an unknown make or model. You don't have the plate, and you cannot tell me what the suspects look like. This happened earlier today, and no one is currently on the scene at the log dump, correct?

Male Caller: Correct.

Dispatch: I'm not sure how I can help you with this.

Male Caller: You can solve the situation.

September 9TH, 2016 – 12 Hour Shift

Dear Jackson, I hate your stinking guts. You make me vomit. You're scum beneath my toes. Love, Audrey." I read my email out loud to Jon and Megan. [1]

"Wow, Audrey wrote that in an email?" asked Megan. Oh, sweet Megan.

Audrey was eavesdropping on the conversation. "That's not what I sent. I sent an email notification of Mandatory Overtime for next week."

"Yeah, well, it reads the same," I said, shouting across the room. I returned to my desk and scanned my CAD to relieve Megan for her break.

"It's pretty much as you see there," said Megan. She packed up her stuff. "Except, we have been getting calls from Gertrude. Bye!"

---

[1] Little rascals is one of my favorite movies, because I too, am a little rascal.

"Noooooooooooooo," I screamed as Megan ran away, laughing right out of the room.

Every call center has its daily callers, their random "crazies" who report things they imagine, or sometimes the voice in their head relayed the emergency to them. This is just an unpleasant fact.

One of our daily callers is Gertrude.

Gertrude is an elderly woman who had experienced a lot in her lifetime, including a lobotomy in the 50s when they were all the rage. As a general rule, she has a sweet demeanor. However, she is an absolute disruption to the call center.

Many of her complaints are entirely unfounded. For example, she called one day to report that her neighbors were sneaking into her apartment and poisoning her milk.

Plausible?

Maybe.

How does she know this?

Her cat told her. Far less plausible now.

Gertrude calls to report a suspicious vehicle in the area. What makes it suspicious?

She's never seen it before.

She calls to report that her brother is trying to kill her. She says he sneaks into her apartment and moves around her pictures to send her a message.

Plausible?

Maybe.

Except, we have received this complaint for many years and have contacted her brother, who lives 2,500 miles away and hasn't seen his sister in more than twenty-five years.

Is it still plausible that he's back in the area and carrying this out?

Maybe, but we won't send an officer to investigate unless she has more concrete evidence than the pictures moving around.

We still have to take all of Gertrude's calls seriously. Every now and again, she reports something which is actually happening. For example, one night, she called to report that her neighbors were fighting. It turns out it was a male vs. female domestic dispute.

What started like one of Gertrude's regular paranoia calls turned more specific than usual. As the details started coming in, I took the information. Then, to my utter surprise, the officers showed up on the scene, and everything she was reporting was one hundred percent accurate.

This is why we take every call on a case-by-case basis and think each through. That night, Gertrude helped save a life. She helped to get a woman away from an abusive husband. But, unfortunately, not every caller with mental health issues is as lovely as Gertrude.

"Dispatch to Charlie-12, contact request, Miss Gertrude 1726 Main Street, details to your screen," I broadcasted.

"Charlie-12, I've spoken with Miss Gertrude at length about her cat's premonitions. She was advised to write them all down and speak to the Sergeant on Monday. Please let the call-takers know." I could hear the exasperation in his voice.

"Copy that."

July 12TH, 2015 – 8 Hour Shift

When a person is in an altered state due to drugs, dementia, schizophrenia, or other mental health reasons, their reality is *their reality*. Nothing you can do or say will make them understand that what they're experiencing is wrong or somehow altered. You can only enter their reality and validate their feelings, which does not mean validating what they see as correct. It means understanding that what they are seeing *they* think is real and validating those emotions.

"I'm sorry the clowns in the road are smiling at you. I can understand how that can make you uncomfortable. Is there any way to avoid seeing them?"

"Ok. Well, I've explained to you several times that we are not going out there," Megan said.

I sat listening to her take the call.

"No, I did not speak to you yesterday. That must have been someone else."

I could see the frustration on Megan's face. I was pretty sure I knew with whom she was speaking.

"Ma'am, I'm going to have to warn you about making threats on a recorded line."

Now I was one hundred percent sure.

"Well, for the last time, I am telling you that we have no calls open at your address. Therefore no officers are going to come out. However, if you keep threatening my staff, we will be forced to send an officer—No. No. Ma'am, I am going to disconnect the line," Megan hung up.

"Ms. Witch?" I grinned, already knowing the answer.

"Oh. My. God!" Megan sighed heavily. "There's no making sense with that woman. This time though, she didn't just threaten to kill any deputies that came to her house. This time she said she would bring a gun out here and kill us all!"

"That's new," I said.

"Yeah, I probably should report this one," Megan stood to see the supervisor's desk. "Audrey, could you please come here for a minute?"

Audrey muttered, "You know there *are* other supervisors."

"You should probably listen to the recording of this last call I took. She threatened us all this time." Megan continued explaining her recent phone call.

Ms. Witch—her full name is Wicked Witch of West Valley—is a terrible shrew of a woman. She uses manipulation tactics to get what she wants. While I don't know her official diagnosis, she makes it hard to care.

Ms. Witch will call her bank, insurance company, Chase Visa, and other businesses to request silly things. When they refuse to give in to her wishes, Ms. Witch informs them she will kill herself. The general policy of these companies is to call 911 and report a suicidal subject. It is then our policy to take the report of a suicidal caller seriously and send the police to their location to resolve the situation and get help to the suicidal subject.

Unfortunately, this is not where it ends.

Ms. Witch has a sordid history with law enforcement, and she hates every last one of them. So when she makes her suicidal call to whichever company is lucky enough to be harassed that day, we are called. We have to send the police per policy. The police arrive at her door, and she turns absolutely violent. Ms. Witch kicks, screams, yells, threatens, and insists she is not suicidal and wants the cops to leave her property and never return. Which is fine by the police, so they go.

It does not end there, either.

Ms. Witch proceeds to tie up 911 lines, informing us how un-suicidal she is. For several hours and sometimes days, she must repeatedly let us know she doesn't need assistance. She reminds us that she does not want the police called to her house, ever, ever, ever again.

Rationality and reason do not apply to Ms. Witch. We explain to her that in order for us not to send the police, she has to stop telling companies she is suicidal. We've presented this to her several ways, but unfortunately, it does not click logically in her head. She simply cannot comprehend why she should stop making empty threats.

It is a vicious circle. Around, and around, and around.

We clarified with Ms. Witch—she told us she was not suicidal. She won't harm the police or herself, so there's no sense in calling us.

It does not matter.

We listen to the entire rant, waiting for *her* to hang up. If we hang up first, she will call right back.

Law enforcement has been down several avenues with this individual. They started addressing the legal ramifications of calling 911 without an emergency and charged her with false reporting. Ms. Witch went to jail—not easily. She physically fought with the police. She then urinated on the officer while being arrested.[2] It temporarily solved the 911 line issue until she was out and started the whole scenario again.

It seemed Ms. Witch finally understood that abuse of the 911 line would get her arrested. That is until she discovered the non-emergency line. This line does not have the same rules as the 911 lines. So instead of tying up the 911 lines, a criminal offense, she'd bug us on the non-emergency line, something we can do nothing about.

Officers attempted an Involuntary Mental Health Treatment, also known as an ITA. However, it also failed to stick. Ms. Witch went away to a mental health clinic for a short while, but she was back like a stray cat.

"Wow, Megan, you got her spun up this time," Audrey said loud enough for the whole room to hear. "This is the first time Ms. Witch specifically stated she would come into the sheriff's office and kill specific individuals, including us."

"I didn't mean to," Megan said. Genuine concern washed over her.

"I am just kidding about you specifically spinning her up. It was not anything you did," Audrey assured her. "I've personally said worse to her. I've been dealing with her for years, and she still gets under my skin. But, unfortunately,

---

[2] I asked how she managed to contort over his leg. He didn't want to explain.

none of us have the coping mechanisms to deal with this one."

"I do," I said. "Ms. Witch and I are on a bowling team together. We're called the Homicidal Head Pins."

"Shut up, Jackson," everyone said in unison.

Audrey took the recording and reported it to the sheriff's office, which prepared to take the information to the courts and officially charge Ms. Witch with a felony threat to kill. The next day, our neighboring agency called to advise us that she was in a pawnshop trying to purchase a handgun. Thankfully this stepped up the efforts to detain her.

Luckily, she was not allowed to purchase a gun. Ms. Witch was taken into custody, not without incident. She still put up a physical fight with the arresting officers, proceeded to urinate on the officers once more, and this time even defecated herself.[3]

As the years passed with Ms. Witch, we moved to a more hands-off strategy. We still take the reports of her suicidal calls from various businesses. However, we only dispatch them to a captain who takes the CFS from there. Unless we get a specific threat of means, time, et cetera for the suicide, we do not respond. This has become our new protocol for Ms. Witch. The incidences involving Ms. Witch have steadily declined, but she is still out there, haunting the West Valley.

---

[3] I know you love the poo stories. It got everywhere in the cruiser. The officer had to open both back doors and spray the feces out. Bet he didn't learn that trick at the academy.

October 14TH, 2015 – 12 Hour Shift

We have a never-ending number of frequent callers. The people who want to report crimes they *believe* are happening. Sometimes we even get sucked into the story. They build it up as if it's real—because let's not forget, to them, it is real.

At least once a month, we receive a phone call from such a woman. She weaves a convincing story about her intelligence of a local crime ring. Then, she will start naming names and addresses. Usually, the addresses will verify, and the people sound plausible. It's only after she's convinced someone of a new story that it turns into a tale worthy of a sci-fi novel.

Our fair city was, in fact, the landing spot for an alien invasion. These aliens are Draconian, blood-sucking lizard people who can eat a person's insides and then wear their skin as a suit. The Draconian walks around just like you and me. Undetectable by the naked eye. They are here to take over the world. President Obama is one. They have infiltrated all levels of government, including law enforcement. If we do not publicly share the documents, evidence of the landing, and an apology for holding on to the information, she will sue the entire county.

"Who knows? Maybe she is on to something," I said. "Maybe I am a lizard person?"

"I think you'd make a terrific lizard person," Pam said a little too enthusiastically.

"Thank you, Pam. You could be one too. I've seen your scaly elbows," I only half-joked.

"Nope, you're not a lizard person. You're just a regular asshole. At least lizard people have desires to infiltrate governments. Your greatest desire in life is to annoy me," Pam said.

"A task I take very seriously."

May 23RD, 2014 – 12 Hour Shift

Bill is another man whose reality is split. Into what sections, I'm still not sure. Bill causes a particular problem for 911 when he calls to report a dangerous crime happening in full view of his downtown apartment.

Every scenario Bill calls about is entirely plausible. We are always met with incredibly detailed descriptions of events. Each one of his calls is also wholly fabricated in his head. Bill can see details and report the suspect's clothing and physical descriptions, vehicle make, model, and plate. For example, he's called to report a woman being sexually abused behind the restaurant across the street from his apartment. He gave us a detailed description of the female and her two assailants.

Law enforcement got on the scene, and there was no one there.

Could the suspects have possibly escaped before law enforcement got on the scene?

Nope. Even when the police arrived, Bill still saw the suspects. In fact, law enforcement was standing right next to them.

The solution was to move Bill's apartment to another side of the building. The thought was that the false reports would stop without a view of a populated area. Perhaps he would have some peace as well. The Chief of Police worked with the local housing authority and got his apartment reassigned.[4]

This backfired, though. Bill's new apartment had a water view. So now, he called in to report boats on fire, bodies floating in the water, injured animals, and poaching.

These reports garnered a much larger response, including law enforcement and the fire department. With such significant and costly responses executed several times a week, a more permanent solution became necessary.

"Ok, Bill. Now are you sure you're seeing this with your human eyes?" asked Jon.

I laughed in the background. Sometimes Jon says things on the 911 line that are wildly inappropriate. For instance, a caller once reported finding needles on the ground in front of her house on the sidewalk. Jon tells the RP, "Sure, ma'am, I'll have an officer come by, pick up those needles and throw them in the garbage for you."

Jon disconnected the line with Bill.

"Human eyes?" I asked.

"Yeah," Jon explained. "It's a system I've worked out with him."

"Does it work?"

---

[4] If it wasn't immediately clear, Bill lived in government subsidized housing, which is why they were able to move him. I wish I had the authority to just move anyone. My neighbors with the barking dog would be elsewhere.

"For the most part," Jon said. "You know he reports the craziest shit, right? Well, I asked him one day why he believed it was happening. I tried to get to the root of the issue. Well, apparently, an Angel speaks to him and tells him about it."

"Are those his unhuman eyes then?"

"Correct. If he sees it in Angel's eyes, I can ascertain that this is most likely not occurring," Jon looked quite smug.

"Sometimes, I can't tell if you're crazy or genius," I said.

Jon is absolutely the worst dispatcher we have. He is a liability waiting to happen. The way he treats people on the phone, he misses radio traffic, and the fact that he does not care much about policy and procedure is abhorrent.

Jon is my absolute favorite coworker.

He makes up for what he lacks in dispatcher abilities in pure entertainment. I can say this because I do not supervise him.

Jon called one of the sergeants and explained Bill's human eyes versus when he's seeing through Angel's eyes. He explained how successful the *human eyes* system had been. Together, the sergeant and Bill came up with a similar approach to help Bill tell if something was in his head or not. Bill now reports what he sees with his Angel's eyes during the day, in person, at the police department. This saves the calls from going to 911. Bill speaks directly to the on-duty sergeant. His concerns are validated, but resources aren't needlessly wasted on his visions.

It is rumored that Bill has been prescribed a new medication. Vindicated by the fact the calls for large-scale, in-progress emergencies have steadily declined.

We still do get the odd call about bald eagles stuck in fishing nets from time to time. We recognize that it is Bill calling, ask him about which eyes are seeing it, send a single resource to get eyes on the potential situation, and go from there.

Leave it to Jon, the worst of the worst, to develop a more permanent solution. A broken clock is still right two times a day.

July 27TH, 2014 – 8 Hour Shift

Did you see the new hires in the classroom when you came in?" I asked Jon as I sat down at my desk.

"No," he spun around. "Any hotties?"

"Are there ever any?" I asked.

"Negative. I think it's a rule that we all have to be a certain level of homely if we want this job," Jon chuckled.

"That could be true. They stick us in this room with no windows, don't let us see people face to face, and we barely see the outside."

"You think that's an accident? Quasimodo did not choose to be kept in the bell tower," Jon laughed.

"True. Anyway, back to my initial point of this whole encounter. I saw the new recruits today. Tana called me in to say hello."

"Why?" Jon asked. "Not exactly the smartest idea if you want to make a good impression on the new people to bring in a graveyard worker."

"I couldn't agree more. Tana asked me to speak to the class quickly and answer their questions. I agreed. They asked me the usual stuff, like if I liked it here. I lied and said *it was great*. They asked if I get much overtime, and I said *yep, which is why I need all of you rockstars to work extra hard to get through this class and ease the burden*. They looked at each other, wondering if I was joking," I widened my eyes and looked from side to side, mimicking them. "I love their innocent little faces, so full of hope and potential."

"Wait until they take their first call like I had earlier on my overtime shift," Jon said.

"Oh? What'd you have?"

"Oh, I kept the tape. I knew you'd love it. Check your email," he pointed to my computer screen. I logged in and clicked open the email from Jon. It was titled 'Interesting Sexual Assault.' I was intrigued.

I opened the attachment and pressed play.

The recording clicked to life. "911, where is your emergency?" Jon said.

"Over at the Apartments at Grey's Park," said a man with a raspy voice.

"Ok, and what are you reporting?" Jon asks.

"I was just sexually assaulted," said the man in an even tone.

"Ok, is the person who did this still there?" Jon asked.

"No."

"When did this occur?"

"Just a few minutes ago, when he flew over," the man said.

Aside from his voice sounding a little raspy, there were no immediate indicators of intoxication.

"When he did what?" Jon asked.

I would have also asked him the same thing.

"He flew over."

"Flew over what?"

I could imagine Jon, at this point, looking up the call history for this phone number.

"He flew over my house and sexually assaulted me," the man said.

The RP was still holding a normal conversational tone. Usually, you can tell at this point in a call if a person is suffering some mental health issues. Their voices are generally higher pitched, they have rapid speech with very few pauses, and they're often unable to concentrate long enough to answer a question precisely. There are other indicators as well, but this man had none.

"How did he fly over your house?" Jon said. I could tell from his tone that Jon was more relaxed now and less concerned about it being an actual emergency.

"In his airplane. These men fly over my house in their airplanes and send down laser beams at my genitals and rape me," the RP continued, "This keeps happening to me, and I'm sick of it. I've written a letter to Delta Airlines about it, but they just think I'm crazy."

"All right, do you want to see an officer in person tonight to report all of this?" Jon asked.

"Yes."

Jon got his name and phone number, letting him know the next steps. I stopped the recording and closed out the email. I looked over at Jon and shook my head.

"Wow. I would like to say I'm surprised, but I'm not," I said. "No one ever molests me from an airplane. I'm a little jealous."

"No one ever molests you ever, I'd guess," Jon said, turning around. I didn't even have a comeback. I sat in my burn because it was so very—true.

Working this job leaves little time for dating. We tend to get married to the job. The other prevalent option was dating the responders. Dispatchers have a long tradition of dating cops, often married ones. We have nicknames for these people; badge bunnies, cop-tarts, pig pals, holster sniffers, holster honeys, hero chasers, and my favorite: hose hoes—for the ones who prefer firefighters.

Between the hours we work, the vast amount of overtime, and the type of work we do, it essentially kills our social life. However, many develop deeper friendships and bonds within the dispatch center or with the responders. In addition, we all tend to have a similar sense of humor and can laugh at the macabre, which isn't appropriate dinner-party talk with people not in the industry.

I remember the first time I had a significant family event after starting at the 911 center. Everyone was curious about my job and wanted a fun 911 story. So I told them about this woman who had killed herself in the bathtub. Before I even got the punchline of the funny story, I looked around at everyone's faces, only they were faces of sadness--Not intrigue.

I quickly changed it to a sad story of how the poor woman killed herself on Christmas by drowning in the tub, and we did not find her body until January 3rd. I looked around, and they shared comments like "Oh no, poor lady" and "Wow, that's horrible."

I didn't even get to the part where she had left the water running and flooded the entire house, and that's how we found her. It had filled up the garage and started spilling down the driveway. I did not tell them how perfectly preserved her body was because of the cold fresh water and how different it was from a body in a lake or the ocean. I also didn't get to tell them how upset the cops were because the water was deep enough to spill over the top of their boots and soak their socks. They would have to slosh around for the rest of the night.

January 7TH, 2012 – 12 Hour Shift

One Saturday morning, we took a call from a 6-year-old girl, Millie. Millie was reporting her mother fell down the stairs. But unfortunately, her mom wasn't waking up, and worse, Millie was trapped under her mom.

With an open line, we could also ascertain Millie was injured. She explained her head and her arm hurt. We kept the line open until the fire department got on the scene. When they arrived, they were utterly befuddled. A conscious and alert patient was at the bottom of the stairs, as reported. However, Millie was nowhere to be found.

The firefighter searched the entire residence for the 6-year-old girl who called 911. Millie was actually Rebecca, a 42-year-old woman diagnosed with Dissociative Identity Disorder also known as Multiple Personality Disorder. [5] During the trauma of the fall, one of her alternative personalities took the stage of her awareness. Millie called 911 to protect the host, who was unable to call herself.

Each call center has its own struggle with mental health callers. This is not just a problem for law enforcement. These people have a resounding effect on hospitals, public transit authorities, local businesses, free clinics, etc. I could go on and on about health care in the United States or lack thereof.

I'm going to spare you my rant.

I think we all know the problems. I don't see the solution, but I'm afraid I think it will get worse before it gets any better.

I never spoke with Millie or Rebecca a second time. Once again, proving that not all who have mental health issues are a burden on the system. All are deserving of the benefit of the doubt. Millie and Rebecca have genuine medical concerns, and although they struggled to communicate their needs, we were able to get them the help they deserved.

[5] Folks diagnosed with DID have two or more separate identities. These individual personalities control the host's behavior at different times. Each identity has a personal history, traits, likes, and dislikes.

March 15TH, 2018 – 12 Hour Shift

My husband is kind of famous, and so I'm afraid this woman outside of my house might be a crazed fan," said the middle-aged RP.

Of course, he is, lady… I thought indignantly. I took down her information. As I pulled up the address into the CAD system, I noticed an open call at the same address.

The other CFS was a welfare check on a male located at the same residence. That RP was also a woman. She called, saying she purchased "something" for the male, and he was not answering his door. She was concerned because she hadn't heard from him in a while. The RP knew he lived there with his wife and stated that the couple knew she would be showing up that night.

Still speaking with the wife who called me, I realized there really was an unknown woman at her front gate. While I was getting information about the middle-aged woman and her husband, I quickly googled the names she gave. Sure enough, I got re-directed to her husband's Wikipedia link. He was, in fact, the drummer for a major band. His name matched the name registered to the house.

This, indeed, was a crazed fan outside of their home.

I honestly did not believe this type of stuff happened.

The officer responding to the incident was delayed by a higher-priority call.

Twenty or so minutes later, the same number rang again. But, this time, it was the actual drummer himself!

Trying to maintain my calm, professional demeanor, I took his call. He was a charming man. He understood the reason for the delay and stated he would be releasing his guard dogs into the yard, as a precaution. He advised that the dogs would not distinguish law enforcement from a crazed fan running through the property, so he requested we call him before arriving on the scene so he could call them inside.

I was completely star-struck.

He just gave me his phone number!

Stay professional, Jackson.

After the officer cleared his priority incident, I asked him to call me. Trying to keep my composure on the phone, it became quickly evident the officer was also a fan of this band and was fangirling harder than I was.

"So, you actually got to talk to him?" the officer perked up.

"Yeah! His wife called first and I spoke to her. The woman requesting the welfare check aka the suspect, called before the both of them, but I did not take the previous call."

"Did he seem cool?"

"Way cool, dude," I casually explained as though the drummer and I were old chums.

"So, does he want contact from me then?" It was hilarious listening to a 45-year-old burly police officer geek out like a 14-year-old girl at a Taylor Swift concert.

"Yes sir, but I think he probably wants you to do an area check for the weirdo at his gate first." I reminded.

"Right, right, right. Of course. Then I am supposed to knock on his door?" he clearly forgot how to do his job.

"No dude, I got his phone number. Don't go inside the property line. He's got his guard dogs patrolling," I explained.

"Well, of course, he has attack dogs. That just makes sense!"

"Are you on your way yet?" I asked.

"Oh yeah—I've been en route this entire conversation," the officer said. "I wonder if it would be unprofessional to get an autograph."

"Yes, it probably would be." I laughed and ended the phone call.

The officer got on the scene of the residence and did a perimeter check for the female suspect. She was long gone. Likely due to the time delay of the officers and realizing she'd been discovered. The dogs may have also contributed to this.

The officer called me back after the whole ordeal. He explained the drummer received several strange Facebook, Instagram, and emails from this woman. She was a crazed fan who decided they were meant to be together, despite his marriage.

We did a little research on the female. The name she gave was fake. The phone number she used to call 911 provided an address but no name. A little research on the in-house address returned two possible women. We looked both up for a criminal record but came up null.

I never found out how the ordeal ended, if the officer ever figured out who she was or charged her with a crime.

Sometimes, it is a part of the job not knowing how things pan out.

To give you a sense of what it feels like, I am not going to tell you who this famous person was.

Plus, my lawyer says I can't.

4
Breaking The Rules Can Be Pawsitively Life-Changing

Dispatch: 911, where is your emergency?

Female Caller: Yes, I'm out on Dispatch Road, and a herd of cows is in the roadway.

Dispatch: Ok, how many cows are there?

Female Caller: I see five, there are two more on the side of the road, but there are five definitely in the roadway. There's a curve right before here, and the speed limit is 55. If someone came around the corner too fast, they might not see them in time.

Dispatch: Ok, can you see where they possibly belong?

Female Caller: Yes, I think they are supposed to be in this field right here. It appears a part of the fence broke, and they just got out. Oh no—

Dispatch: What?

Female Caller: A semi-truck is coming, and he doesn't seem to be slowing down. I don't think he sees them, and oooooooooooooh my god—

Dispatch: Did he hit one?

Female Caller: Nope, he hit all five of them. You better get someone over here; I don't think some of them are dead.

Animal calls are a special type of call in dispatch centers. Mine was no exception. We have a limited Animal Control program that employs one man. The Animal Control Officer works Monday through Friday during business hours. He only handles domesticated animals.

We have a Fish and Wildlife Department, but they only deal with poachers and dangerous animals in residential areas, such as a bear or cougars. Within our agency, any other type of animal call isn't going to be resolved when you call 911.

There are a few exceptions. We will send an officer to the scene if the animal impedes traffic. Officers really dislike being called out to these types of calls. It usually involves the officer scraping some sort of animal pelt off the middle of the roadway and dragging it securely onto the side of the road and out of the way of traffic.

"You know, when I first started here, the meat used to be collected and served to the inmates of our county jail." I can never tell if Jon is joking with me or if that used to be how they did it back in the yesteryears. "I'll let your mind wander with that one."

"You're disgusting."

Domesticated animal issues are usually relatively simple to handle. For example, dog complaints are almost exclusively about excessive barking. If the call is about a cat, it's usually lost or occasionally up a tree. If the call is about a horse or cow, it's inevitably in the roadway. Smaller animals, such as opossums or raccoons, are classified as pests and are up to the individual to call an exterminator.

"I used to have a pet seal," Jon said.

I cannot deal with him today. Occasionally, we get strange calls we don't know what to do with.

"Ok, how did you have a pet seal?" Jon's messing with me, but I'm compelled to play his game.

"He just hung out in the backyard. He lived in the shed. We named him Muffin. He was a sweetheart," Jon said, stone-cold.

"Seals are aquatic animals. How did you have it living in your shed?"

"We had a little water tank for him to swim in." His face never wavers.

I don't know how to take him sometimes.

January 10ᵀᴴ, 2018 – 8 Hour Shift

I live in a coastal community where the occasional baby seal call is not unusual to stumble upon. Elephant seals come onto the beach to molt. They wiggle around, and to some, they look injured. This is a natural process. There isn't anything human interaction can help with. They are perfectly ok and need to be left alone. This doesn't, however, prevent folks from calling 911 in hopes of rescuing these seals. Luckily, there is a seal, whale, and otter hotline that we can refer callers to if they have further questions.

"Ma'am, if you would just listen for a mome—"

Jon is on with a caller, and my spidey senses are tingling.

"Ma'am, I told you. If you jus—"

He really doesn't like being cut off.

"Uh-huh. Yep. I understand—"

This goes on for a while.

"Yes, ok. Alright, are you ready to listen to me now? No. I've listened to you for eight minutes now. You can listen to me for 30 seconds. The seal is fine. This is a natural process. When the mo—"

Here it comes.

"Ma'am, just like with human children, they miss their moms when they're gone. They scream and cry until she returns. Seals are no different. The mother seal is out hunting and will return to her crying baby in due time. But, unlike your children who never call, this baby actually misses its mother." Jon hangs up.

"You're going to get fired." I'm too stunned to say much else.

"You promise?"

Another ubiquitous animal call for our 911 center is about deer. The deer has a broken leg, is eating their favorite plants, appears undernourished, has two fawns with it, or my personal favorite, the deer with the fractured jaw that has its tongue hanging out. I named her Silly-Sally. Silly-Sally became a legend in my center. We would take bets on how many calls in a week we would get about Silly-Sally. I won $15.

There is absolutely nothing that we can do for a deer. If a deer has been struck by a vehicle, law enforcement will respond to "dispatch" the animal nine times out of ten. Translation—the deer is shot in the head by a police officer to end its suffering.

The people in my small town find this appalling. So apparently, Bambi was a big hit?

I'm not sure.

Either way, they always feel that something should be done. Why isn't there an injured deer emergency room somewhere? They want the Bambilence called[1]. Good luck getting that funded.

It's always tricky to explain these hard facts to panicked RPs. So we do our best to avoid the question: What will *happen to the deer?* In lieu of answering, we let the officer explain when he arrives.

Admittedly, sometimes when I'm feeling particularly malicious, I'll enjoy explaining to the person that poor little Bambi will be at the receiving end of a 9mm pistol. As I mentioned, you must be slightly sadistic to survive in this industry.[2]

Just keeping hold of that perspective.

Dr. Tony, a local veterinarian, had a reputation for taking in the occasional injured wildlife. He would rehabilitate them and then release them into the wild once more. One night, a woman called 911 to report an injured deer along the highway, and she wanted it taken to Dr. Tony, who would *fix him up.* We transferred her to the State Patrol. All calls taking place on a highway are their jurisdiction.

The RP called back several times. Each conversation would end by transferring her to State Patrol. After an hour or so, she called back extremely upset and demanded to speak with the sergeant at the State Patrol. Later that evening, the State Patrol Trooper swung by the dispatch center, and we asked him about the deer going to Dr. Tony.

---

[1] Get it? Bambilence, because it's an ambulance for Bambi.
[2] In case you're still not understanding, the officer will shoot the deer in the head… Bam. Dead.

The trooper laughed. "I got out there, and the woman was stuffing a deer carcass into her tiny Toyota Yaris.[3] The deer was quite deceased and partially decomposed."

"No way!" This trooper wasn't the type to exaggerate.

"I told her that this deer was exceptionally dead and there would be nothing Dr. Tony could do for it. It took me nearly 20 minutes to convince this woman that she needed to leave the deer carcass on the roadside and continue with her evening."

"Did you do the scientific poke test in the eye with your knight stick?" Jon asked eagerly.

The trooper laughed and took that as his cue to exit.

We shared the funny story with our coworkers when the next shift came on. That's when they informed us that not only was this woman crazy for trying to save an obviously dead deer, Dr. Tony had been dead for several years.

Maybe Dr. Tony was treating this deer in the afterlife.

April 20TH, 2014 – 8 Hour Shift

Back in the early 90s, there was what some news outlets called an "epidemic of rabid bats" plaguing parts of the country. I don't believe that it was an actual epidemic. But, if I remember correctly, some young girl somewhere in the Midwest got bit by a bat, and it must have been a slow news week because every freaking news source picked up the story and ran with it.

---

[3] The smallest car they make. If you don't know it, Google it , it's worth the mental image.

Everywhere people seemed to be absolutely infatuated with rabid bats. You had to be careful because these flying monsters were carrying disease and were definitely out to get you with their rabies. I don't remember if the girl lived or died from contracting rabies, but it doesn't matter. The legacy has carried on. People are stupidly afraid of bats. To this day, news stories like this lead folks to believe the government or law enforcement agencies care about bats.

I'm here to tell you, as an experienced 911 dispatcher, we do not care about bats, and no local agencies oversee them. So unless you live next door to an actual outbreak, chances are your bat worries are unfounded. I know that as you're reading this, you are thinking of your personal story of your cousin's friend from Austin who got rabies from a bat.

Whatever.

I don't believe you either.

A man called 911 early into one of my overnight shifts about a bat that "probably" had rabies. The RP explains the bat crashed out of the sky and almost landed on him. It rolled under his barbeque grill, and the RP secured the bat in a plastic bag. He insisted that the health department be dispatched to him immediately to retrieve this rabid bat.

Sometimes it's easier to just let people ramble than try to stop them to acquire the relevant information needed[4]. After listening to his long story, I attempted to find the emergency in his call. "Did the bat bite or scratch anyone?"

"No."

---

[4] The location of where the RP is at being the exception of course. It should always, always, always comes first.

"The only way anyone could have contracted rabies from the bat is if it bit or scratched someone." Unfortunately, for both of us, this did not register with the RP. Clearly, I was the crazy one. How could the health department not care about a RABID BAT?

I tried to turn the conversation around to make him see that he was being unreasonable. This never actually works, but somehow, it makes me feel like I've tried. I asked, "How do you know the bat was rabid in the first place?"

"It fell out of the sky in the daylight," although it was near sunset by my own approximations. "The only rational explanation for his fall would be it has rabies," he explained.

I tried to offer him some alternatives. "Perhaps it was attacked by something and was killed in the air? Maybe it was just old? It could have choked on a bug and suffocated? Just because it fell doesn't prove without a doubt that it has rabies."

I continued to try to explain, "Even if it did, in fact, have rabies, unless it bit a human being, there really isn't anything we can do. No agency in our entire state would care about the bat if it hasn't harmed anything or anyone."

"What am I supposed to do with the carcass then?"

That is a fair question. Finally, I seemed to be getting through. But, unfortunately, I could already tell he wouldn't like my answer.

"Since it is already in a bag, go ahead and dispose of it in the trash."

He started to spin up.

"You can also burn or bury it. Whatever you feel is necessary," because ultimately, it didn't matter.

This entire conversation was not good enough; he demanded to speak to a supervisor. So I put him on hold.

"Ooooooooooh, Audrey."

She looked at me like a disappointed mother looks at their child who just got arrested.[5]

Audrey told the man the same thing I did.

September 19TH, 2016 – 12 Hour Shift

Jackson, when you take the Police 2 frequency, I need you to stop saying that you have *dropped the deuce in your ear*," Audrey says, trying to kill all my joy.

"Have there been complaints?" I asked.

"Yes. From me, it's gross." Audrey said.

I laughed and turned around to look at my workload.

The policy of the agencies I serve is that an animal does not receive special treatment. Law enforcement in our area is for protecting human life.

There is the exception, of course, of the Animal Control Officer who deals with animal cruelty claims and other domesticated animal complaints and concerns. It is a rare case that an officer will take time out of their schedule to save an animal's life. Not because they don't care about animals but

---

[5] Working next door to the jail, I've seen this look on more than a few occasions.

because the priority needs to be human life and property. They often wish they could do something.

As an animal lover, I can certainly sympathize with a caller concerned for a creature's well-being. Unfortunately, the policies of the agencies I represent have the final word. I have the pleasure of telling folks that there is nothing that we can do. Ultimately, it is up to the private citizen to find after-hours care for any animal they take in. They are also on the hook for the bill.

No one ever likes that answer, but it's the truth.

On extremely rare occasions, we get to save an animal. One such example is when I got to rescue a Saint Bernard.

The call came in at approximately 10 p.m., far beyond when Animal Control could assist.

The reporting party stated that an older-looking Saint Bernard was in the middle of a private road, lying in a mud puddle with a little Chihuahua by its side. The RP stated she attempted to assist the dog and get him out of the roadway, but the dog was too weak and injured to move.

There are two problems with this scenario.

The first is that this call was about an injured animal. Once again, it was the policy of the police agency that they would not respond. Two, the dog was on a private road. I cannot assign it as a traffic complaint since the road did not belong to the county. My hands were pretty tied on the subject. I explained this to the caller, and she was responsive and understanding.

I don't know why, but I had to break policy and save this dog.

Everything in me said to save them.

Thankfully, it was a particularly slow night, and one of my good friends was on patrol that night. I asked her to call me on the un-recorded line.[6]

"Is this Alexandra, the most awesome, amazing, awe-inspiring officer in the entire world?" I had to butter her up.

"What do you want?"

I explained what was going on. Alex graciously agreed to head over and see what she could do.

In the meantime, I attempted to get a hold of a friend of a friend who ran the local animal rescue clinic. I explained the situation to her and expounded that I could not authorize any sort of payment from the county or any agency to assist with the animal.

The clinic manager was also sympathetic to my concern. As luck would have it, an employee of hers lived right up the road from the incident. The clinic manager told me she would try to see if her employee would volunteer to go and help the animals.

Thankfully, she was available!

The employee, a veterinarian, was on the scene within five minutes. Between the four of us, we were able to find the owner of the dog. They were extremely grateful to everyone involved. We saved a Saint Bernard that day, off the books of course[7].

---

[6] The unrecorded line doesn't exist at every agency, so know before you go annoy your local 911 center about it.

[7] This is the real reason I had to change all of our names for this book.

October 14TH, 2018 – 12 Hour Shift

Many dispatch centers have secondary centers. These are for specific agencies that have their own departments. One such example is the State Patrol. They have different policies, styles of policing, and specific jurisdictions. Therefore, anything that happens on a highway belongs to them. Their main focuses are speeding tickets, traffic collisions, and DUIs.

State Patrol tends to get stumped when cases fall outside of these lines. This is a source of amusement for me, as we can silently monitor calls we've transferred to them.

This particular animal call came in pretty late into the evening. Animal Control was long gone. Fish and Wildlife hadn't had a unit in service for several hours, and I knew that this call would throw State Patrol through a loop. I decided to stay on the line and listen in case I could help.

At worst, I'd get to laugh at them while they struggled.

I have a problem.

I can admit it.

The RP was very agitated prior to when the State Patrol call-taker started their line of questioning. First, the call-taker asked about the emergency location[8]. The RP stated an injured owl was sitting in the middle of the highway. The RP insisted that someone saves the owl before a semi-truck comes through and "murdered this majestic creature."

State Patrol went through the usual questions: How do you know the owl is injured? Why do you believe it won't fly away if a truck comes by? Etc.

Unfortunately, this line of questioning made the RP even more agitated. After all, why wouldn't an officer just come with lights and sirens blaring?

Save this poor, innocent owl's life!

Clearly, the call-taker was an animal-hating Nazi[9].

At this point in the conversation, I'm giggling so hard with the mute button firmly pressed[10]

State Patrol tries to explain that nature needs to run its course, and an officer would not be responding to the owl.

This infuriates the RP, who promptly demands to speak with a supervisor. The supervisor gets on the line and goes over all of the same information again with the RP. The supervisor repeats, verbatim, what the call-taker said. Finally, in a last-ditch effort, the supervisor suggests to the RP that she be the hero and move the owl off to the side of the road.

The RP asks the supervisor, "Won't it bite me?"

To which the supervisor replied, "Uhm, yeah, probably."

---

[8] A+ on their part!

[9] Don't look at me that way. This is a healthy use of sarcasm!

[10] Oh yes, there is a mute button. It has saved my career on many occasions. Too many to count.

I was laughing out loud, full belly, rolling, laughing. My partner that night was Megan, and she thought I was crazy. I could not wait to playback the recording for her.

The supervisor finally terminated the call, and I never found out what happened to the owl or the RP's fingers.

Megan doubted the RP got her fingers bit.

"How do you know?" I asked.

"I'd be sending the ambulance by now."

June 2ND, 2019 – 12 Hour Shift

Cats are admittedly not my favorite animal. I am much more of a dog person. However, when it comes to an animal in need of any species, I am a sucker and will try to assist where I can. I did not know what to make of this call. It came across my screen near the beginning of my shift. I honestly thought the call-taker was messing with me at first.

"Really, Jon?" I asked as he walked by my desk, presumably on his way to his break.

"What?" He knows what.

"This cat call?"

"Haha. I thought you might like that one."

"I don't even know what I'm supposed to do with it. They didn't want an ambulance for the scratches?" I asked. Trying to figure out how to put this call out on the radio.

"No. I asked! Be glad I didn't put it in as a burglary in progress." He chuckled and watched me read and re-read this call.

"Isn't that already a thing? A cat burglar? It sounds familiar." I continued reading. "They've locked *themselves* in the bathroom? I initially read it as they locked the cat in there."

"No, they are definitely stuck. I ultimately decided to put it in rather than tell them to figure it out." He wasn't wrong, but somehow it wasn't right either.[11]

I had to figure this out.

"Ok, well, here goes nothing." I stepped on my pedal and broadcasted, "Charlie 12 and Charlie 14, a dangerous animal call."

"Go ahead."

"1421 88th Street, Apartment 2. Contact RP regarding a stray cat that she and her friend brought home. Apparently, it started out friendly and turned unfriendly. Break." I stepped off the broadcasting pedal. I am apparently going whole ham on this. "The suspect pulled out 10 tiny knives attached to its paw and attacked them. The RP and her friend have now retreated into the bathroom while the suspect is still roaming the apartment."

"Uhhh, copy…"

"Suspect described as being 1 foot tall, 13 pounds, orange, armed with 4 murder mittens complete with 5 knives on each mitten." If you're going to go big, go really big. "Answers to the name of Fluffy"

"Ok. Show us en route."

"And you're going right meow?" I am going to get fired.

---

[11] We have a little rhyme for this, "When in doubt, send them out." It's about liability. The higher-ups in the dispatch center would rather have the police say no than us.

After a few seconds, pause. "Yes, right, meow."

I had Charlie 14 call me at the Comm Center after he'd completed the call. Apparently, the cat returned to its happy state by the time they arrived. They were able to scoop him up without issue. He sat quite happily in the patrol car's front seat on the way to the animal shelter. They had, in fact, appreciated my dispatch too. Apparently, they were in the precinct with several other officers when I dispatched the call, and I got a good chuckle around the room. I'm glad they all took it as the lighthearted joke it was meant to be.

It could have been *cat*astrophic.

5

I Came Here To Save Lives And Make Sandwiches, And I'm All Out Of Mayo

Dispatch: 911, where is your emergency?

Small child: Hello!

Dispatch: Hi there!

Small child: Who is this?

Dispatch: This is 911. Do you know what 911 is?

Small child: No… What are you doing?

Dispatch: I am at work. What about you? What are you doing?

Small child: Playing in my room.

Dispatch: Oh yeah? Is Mom or Dad there with you?

Small child: No…

Dispatch: No? So, you're all alone?

Small child: No…

Dispatch: Well, who is there with you?

Small child: Grandma!

Dispatch: Ok, well, can I talk to Grandma?

Small child: No...

Dispatch: Why not?

Small child: She's asleep and won't wake up.

Dispatch: She won't wake up?

Small child: No.

Dispatch: Can you try to wake her up?

Small child: No.

Dispatch: Why not?

Small child: She'll be mad.

Dispatch: Why will she be mad?

Small child: She said to leave her alone.

Dispatch: Do you know your address?
Small child: No…
Dispatch: *with the mute on* Fucking perfect.

Kid calls are my least favorite calls in the entire world. They trigger me to a place where I am at my most uncomfortable. My head always takes me to the worst possible scenarios. Unfortunately, sometimes that turns into reality.

I know that these calls send my stressors into overdrive. I become fidgety, fumble, diaphoretic, and scatterbrained. Even my heart rate soars. Yet I still have to do my job and stay neutral. I have to remain emotionally and personally out of the call.

In the transcript above, my head instantly went to Grandma is dead. She's dead on the couch, the small child thinks she's "sleeping" and I won't be able to find this girl.

When I pinged the phone's locality, I was able to get an approximate location, reasonably close to where she actually was. However, she lived on the south side of the county while all of my units were up north.

I sat on the phone with this girl, talking about everything from princesses to pizza to fairies and Paw Patrol for 45 minutes until law enforcement arrived.

Thankfully, at the end of the day, Grandma was asleep and did, in fact, tell the juvenile RP to not disturb her.

Law enforcement explained to grandma what had happened and advised her to talk about 911 with her granddaughter—what it is used for, what it is not used for, about what an emergency is, and of course, to the importance of learning her address.

Not all kid calls go so smoothly. It's these calls that live with me, forever burned into the back of my mind.

March 1ST, 2018 – 12 Hour Shift

The father of a five-month-old infant called 911 during my shift. To this day, I can hear his screams of utter horror in my brain if I think about it. An hour before the RP called 911, he put his baby down for a nap. As most parents do, the RP took the opportunity to take a nap. At some point, the baby spit up, aspirated on its vomit, and died. The father was unaware. He, too, was sleeping. He woke to find his child blue and cold. We still went through my usual routine. I acquired all the pertinent information, attempted infant CPR, got the tones out promptly, and ensured the responders got the appropriate information as soon as possible for a timely response.

A paramedic could have been there with him at the time of the call, and it still would have made no difference. The baby was gone.

I take solace in knowing I was there for the father, letting him know that, in those minutes, he did the right thing by calling me and attempting CPR. In those moments, I reassured him that he couldn't have done anything different from that point on. I don't know if my words mattered to him. I'm sure this father would feel guilty for the rest of his life.

Why this father?

Why this baby?

I guess that is just part of life. We never really know how close to death we are.

Gruesome things happen in all walks of life; unfortunately, many of them fall into my lap.

Even though I was not there to see it, I felt it. I relive it. I wonder if there was anything I could have or should have done differently. No other type of call makes me feel as despondent as calls where the child dies.

March 9TH, 2018 – 12 Hour Shift

We had a difficult couple of weeks for infant deaths. Following the tragic loss of the first, two additional children died. The incidents happened one right after another. The same crew was assigned to respond to both, which occurred less than a week apart.[1]

The first call was especially rough.

"You heard about that woman, right?" Pam said after eavesdropping during pass down.

"No," Megan said, glancing up at Pam.

"It was very suspicious circumstances," Pam said. "The paramedics explained that the baby had unusual bruising

---

[1] I've seen so many cosmic coincidences. Out of all the hundreds of potential medics we have in my district, it ended up being the exact same crew again.

around his head. Then, the mother reported that the child acted differently right before she put him to bed.

The paramedics and police asked her several times why she didn't take him to the hospital if she felt things were off. She really didn't have an answer."

Carrie, our fellow dispatcher joined the conversation, "Yeah, right after that, Marc, the medic called me on the radio and asked for police to respond for suspicious circumstances," she said. "I kind of knew something was up, Terrance had the original call, and he said the mom didn't sound bothered at all."

Dispatchers always know when something's up.

"I would be so freaked out. I can't even imagine," Pam said, looking at me specifically. "When my kids were young, like yours, I was on top of every little sniffle, bump, scrape, and bruise like a CSI detective."

"I don't doubt that, Pam," I said. "So, what happened next?"

"Well, Carrie sent the police, and we really don't know much beyond that. It wasn't until a few hours later that we started to get calls from the media. Apparently, they were scanning again and showed up at the house."

"Thankfully, I had Sgt Reyes already there," Carrie said. "You know he's now the media contact."

This was, in fact, news to me. I find it hilarious that the communication part can sometimes be a bit light in a communication center.

The gossip, however, was never in short supply.

"Ok, so what were the other calls?" I asked, hoping this story would end soon so I could start my long-ass shift.

"We got what? Five or six calls to report anonymously, of course, that the mother had been at a party the night before and had dropped the baby and hit its head," Pam said.

"Yeah, I think it was at least five," Carrie said.

"Dang," I said, thinking about this one time when my baby was first born. I was carrying him in this blanket made with silk lining. He slipped out of that thing, and my heart dropped into my butt faster than the inch he moved.

Somehow my ninja dad skills kicked in, and I was able to catch him before he hit the floor. He probably slipped a couple inches from my arms before I caught him. But, in my mind's memory, it felt like that scene from Mission Impossible where Tom Cruise almost hits the ground before the rope catches him.

The guilt I carry to this day for that mini-slip is unreal. I cannot imagine what some of these parents go through after losing a child. I hope I never have to.

Accidents happen.

What upset me is that she did not immediately seek care after he fell. To me, that's negligent.

The mother might have been the cause of this infant's death.

Kid calls are hard enough. Adding negligence just heightens the fear, anger, anxiety, and complex emotions that first responders go through.

The Critical Incident Stress Management (CISM) program assists first responders in the often difficult task of emotionally processing high-stress calls.

The guidelines for an incident to become "critical" are loose. Sometimes, it can be the death of a close friend or family member of a first responder. It can be as large as a mass casualty incident like an active shooter situation. A "critical incident" can be defined as any incident in which emotions run high.

Nearly every communications center has individuals, such as myself, certified in CISM. We are trained to identify specific incidents that may cause heightened stress for first responders. There are sure signs folks start to display, indicating they may have been through a high-stress incident and require stress management skills. These signs often involve alcoholism, distancing themselves from everyday activities, and weight loss or gain.

Each incident is initially assessed for its probability of causing any more than the expected level of stress[2]. In the cases where the potential exists, they are handled through CISM.

The process begins with a *Debriefing*. First responders gather to discuss the incident's facts and emotions. If emotions run high and the facilitators deem it necessary, the group moves into a *Defusing*.

---

[2] Normal being relative. Is it normal to hear people die? I'd say probably not. Unless we're talking about Charles Lee Ray's kill count. 67 during all seven films

Defusing is the emotional aspect of the program. The CISM team treats these similarly to a debriefing. Instead of focusing on the facts of the case, we concentrate primarily on sights, sounds, smells, emotions, thoughts, and feelings. If needed, the next stage would be moving towards one-on-one meetings.

One-on-ones are specialized counseling for an affected individual. In these scenarios, we meet in a small, intimate setting. We remind them of why we do what we do as first responders. It's important to remind individuals that they are not alone and remind them of the importance of self-care and the resources our departments have for them.

CISM is a vital tool for all first responders. 911 dispatchers and call takers are first responders. They deal with the worst of society. We see and hear horrible things on a daily basis. No one calls to talk about happy or invigorating things. They call on the worst days of their lives. They call in the middle of horrific events and tragedies that will scar the RPs for the rest of their lives. As call-takers and dispatchers, we must leave these same terrible events at work and try to continue our personal lives as if nothing is wrong.[3]

It's not so simple, though.

Many of our family members do not understand why we do what we do. They will never be able to comprehend what it's like to do what we do or the emotional toll it carries.

Some of us are lucky enough to have very understanding spouses, parents, friends, et cetera, with whom we can

---

[3] Or we write books to bring you all down with us. Muhahaha!

confide. We are able to talk about the stressors of our jobs. They know to keep an eye on us for warning signs.

While others are "emotional islands" that process internally, we do not have social support at home and rely on our coworkers to recognize signs of struggle.

The severity and stress of the job can be too much for many responders. We are not robots.[4] We feel the weight of every call. Eventually, the compound stress takes over. Many times, we have difficulty recognizing when too much becomes too much. Suicide among first responders is the highest of any other profession globally.

Kid calls tend to affect many responders the most, myself included. After each of the infant deaths, we conducted a debriefing. This is not a program for the public. We have resources for grief counselors, chaplains, and other avenues for the families of the deceased or badly injured. The CISM program is for first responders exclusively. It's another way we care for each other because sometimes the child on the other end of the line is one of our own.

Thankfully, my personal story does not end horribly.

August 7TH, 2014 – 8 Hour Shift

My son was at school like any other day. A woman called 911 to report that a suspicious man was hanging around her students. They were all playing at the playground, and this suspicious man stood watching them, staying in the shadows.

---

[4] That is, until ChatGPT takes our jobs…

After getting as much of a description as possible of the man and the location, I got the caller's information and quickly realized this was *my* son's teacher.

"Holy fuck! This is happening at my son's school," I screamed, hoping I hung up the phone.

"What?" Laura asked from the dispatch terminal.

"Look at 746. That suspicious call at the playground." I pointed to her screen. She had already dispatched the call, thankfully. "That's my kid's class. Miss Adaline called."

"Holy fuck."

"That's exactly what I said. Who do you have going?" I asked. At this point, I have abandoned my call-taking position and have plugged in with the dispatcher. The other call-takers can handle the load for now.

"Charlie 17 and Charlie 12."

"How far away are they? Move the map? Move the map."

She knew I was panicking on the inside and more than a little on the outside.

"Not too far; Charlie 12 was right around the corner on his coffee break when I dispatched him."

"Ahh, I don't like this."

"It's going to be ok. They're going to get there soon," Laura said.

"I know, I know, I know. Come on! Move your ass, Charlie 17!" I said, knowing that Charlie 12 won't move in until his backup is close.

"She hasn't called back, so hopefully, he's still just hanging in the shadows." Laura stayed cool, calm, and collected like a god-damn professional.

"If he fucking touches one hair on one of the heads of any of those kids, I will rip his fucking head off." I wasn't as professional.[5]

"He didn't have any weapons and wasn't even inside the playground," Laura reminded me. "He's skulking outside of it. Which means there's still a lot of distance between them and the suspect."

"I know, but still."

"No, I get it," she moves the map automatically as Charlie 17's car inches closer.[6]

Looking back and reminiscing as I write this, she was great to me then.

Everyone was.

By the time I unplugged and screamed an expletive across the dispatch floor, the rest of the room had sorted everything out. No matter what other call they were working on, every dispatcher in that room was watching that screen. They had their maps fixated the same, watching Charlie 17's GPS car drag towards the scene like I was.

Even my supervisor Mike, who's usually kind of a dick, was silent about me abandoning my post to join Laura.

First and foremost, dispatchers love drama.

I believe that to my core.

They all were invested in the call about my son for the drama and pageantry of it all. The very close second reason is that we have become a giant family in the Comm Center.

---

[5] We're almost 100 pages in, I'm sure you know this already.

[6] To explain this better, we can see their GPS locations albeit slightly delayed. It's like watching your Über Eats driver on your app pick up your McDonalds. See, I know you too…

When something like this happens to one of us, it happens to all of us.

If something horrible were to happen to my son and in-extension to me, it is also in-extension happening to them. They would be the first to assist me in any way possible.

Thankfully, nothing horrible happened to my son that day. However, it does not negate that this man was stalking children, and one of them was *my* child.

It was out of my hands

I could do nothing to get the police there faster.

I could not magic the man away.

All I could do was sit there, hope, and pray that the situation would end well, just like any other call.

After what felt like an eternity, the officers apprehended the individual and removed him from the scene.

I wanted to know what the hell he was doing there.

I wanted to know who he was.

I wanted to know what he had going on his mind. Was he being a creep? Or was there a more innocent reason he was lurking in the shadows of an elementary school? Looking for his lost pet?

The most important thing to me was that my son and his classmates were safe. I know you probably won't believe me, but I never did look up that call.

I don't have the answers. I never asked my son about it. I don't know if he knows anything about this case. He was still relatively young then, so I sincerely doubt it.

He gets to live like most civilians. Never knowing what law enforcement is dealing with right around the corner. Never knowing who or what is lurking in the shadows.

My son was safe that day. I let him keep that.

I have heard tales from other dispatchers that took choking calls, broken limb calls, and traffic collision calls of their own children and families. It is an unfortunate part of the job when you live in the community you serve.

This job can get personal quickly. But, it strengthens the bond between the dispatchers, police officers, and fire department personnel. It clarifies that we all have each other's backs in the community. We treat every call as if we are dealing with our own families because some days, we are.

January 19TH, 2017 – 12 Hour Shift

Some calls are so heinous that I don't like telling people about them.

I think it is general knowledge, but I will reiterate it anyway. Most fire departments have a child-surrender policy if you have an unwanted birth or an unwanted infant. Some have a little mailbox on the side of the building where you can deposit your child, and an alert will sound about thirty seconds after the door is closed, letting the department know that a baby has been dropped off. In some places, it's an outside phone with an emergency button you can press.

I am sure you've heard of children being found in dumpsters or boxes on the side of the roadway.

Unfortunately, they've been found in all sorts of horrible locations.

"I'm sorry, you're hearing what?" Terrance sounded confused and concerned. So, of course, we're all ears.

"What's he got?" I asked Jon. Nothing had come across my dispatch screen yet.

"No idea," Jon went back to his book.

"You don't have anything either?"

Jon looked back at his screen from his book, "Terrance hasn't put anything in yet."

"Is this happening right now?" Terrance questioned the RP.

The suspense is killing me. Jon, however, is cool as a cucumber. He could not care less. I'm sometimes jealous of his ability to disconnect entirely and do the bare minimum.

"Ok, and which side is the front of your house? What street?"

Terrance was starting to piss me off. He didn't have anything in the system yet.

"23rd Avenue?"

Oh. That's going to be my jurisdiction. I turn away from Jon and stare intently at my screen, waiting for Terrance to put his call in.

"Uh-huh, yes, I've got a call already started," Terrance fibbed.

It finally populated on my screen.

CHILD PR/1. A child endangerment. Priority One.

I pull up the call. The narrative read:

>ON THE 23 AV SIDE, RP HEARING A CRYING BABY ON THE FRONT PORCH<

What the hell?

The narrative continued:

>RP TOO SCARED TO CHECK <

"She's afraid of an infant?" I asked out loud to no one in particular.

>RP FEELS IT MAY BE A HOME-INVASION SCAM<

"Oh. I guess that makes a little sense?" I say with thinly veiled sarcasm.

I get on my radio. "Robert 18, Robert 22 for a child endangerment call."

"Go ahead."

"At 2300 Rosebud St on the 23 Avenue side, RP hears what she thinks is a baby crying on her porch. The RP is too afraid to check as she feels it may be a home invasion scam. No weapons mentioned."

"Copy, show us en route."

"Mary 14, show me and Mary 3 also en route to that."

Wow. A sergeant is going too[7].

"Any updates?" Robert 18 asks[8].

"Negative. She is still hearing the baby cry."

The Robert and Mary cars get on the scene. A few minutes pass, and I get a broadcast filled with stifled giggles.

"Robert, 18, we're good here. No baby. If there are any incoming units, they can stand down."

---

[7] Mary 3 is a sergeant
[8] Yes. I have a thousand updates, but I just don't want to tell you.

"Copy."

What the hell? I had to know what was going on. So I messaged Robert 18 on the instant messaging system built into the CAD.

No baby?

Hahaha. Nope. No baby.

What did she hear then?

Two cats making sweet-sweet love.

OMG! LOL!

They took off real quick when we popped around the corner.

I made sure to tell everyone in the Comm Center the outcome since any time there is a CHILD PR/1 call, everyone in the room has it up and monitoring. We had a couple of good laughs as a group.

6
Aliens, UFOs, And Al Qaeda Raccoon

Dispatch: 911, where is your emergency?
Male Caller: Over by the bay.
Dispatch: Ok, and what is going on over by the bay?
Male Caller: Ok, you're going to think I'm crazy, drunk, and I promise I'm neither.
Dispatch: What are you reporting, sir?
Male Caller: I swear to you, as I'm saying this, I understand how crazy it sounds. However, I just saw a UFO, and it looked like it just crash-landed.
Dispatch: Ok, and where does it appear to have crash landed?
Male Caller: In the woods, up the hill from the casino. It was a large flash; a circular craft with lights on it whizzed by, and then a loud thud sound followed by another flash when it crashed down.
Dispatch: Do you see any flames from the impact area?
Male Caller: No, sir, it's too far away to see anything.
Dispatch: What did you say the craft looked like?
Male Caller: It was silver, had whitish/yellow lights on it, and moved like nothing I've ever seen move.
Dispatch: How long was it airborne?
Male Caller: Just a few seconds. It went whirling by. I know you probably think I'm just loony, but I assure you I'm stone–cold sober, and I work on aircraft for a living. I know how they maneuver, what a crash looks like, and what most airplanes look like. This was no ordinary aircraft.
Dispatch: Alright, well, I'll send someone to check into it. Please give us a call back if you see anything else.

I have always wanted a UFO call. [1] They are oddly rare across the 911 circuit. Most callers who report aliens, lizard creatures, or other seemingly extraterrestrial phenomena are in crisis, and the stories always lack any logic. A lot of microwaved genitals, but I'll touch on that later.

Having a seemingly straightforward RP who claims to have seen a UFO is a rare treat. Even more extraordinary to be able to name its current whereabouts.

Unfortunately for me, while the reporting party was within my jurisdiction, the crash site was not. Therefore, I did not get to take this call to completion. The neighboring dispatch agency was good sports about sharing the information with us.

According to their center, the deputy that called for the search was blasé about the whole thing and took his time getting to the crash site. He "searched" the area from his vehicle and cleared it as unfounded.

I may never know if we skirted a first contact situation that night, and the men in black came and covered it all up. But I want to think that's what happened.

My hope is, just like the 1997 classic film "Men in Black" starring Will Smith, the Men in Black got on the scene first. They "flashy-thinged" the deputy, and now he has no memory of finding anything. *Nothing found* is the official report. We may never know for sure.

I personally believe in life beyond Earth, but I doubt we have made first contact. I do not think that there is a major government cover-up. When else in the history of multiple

---

[1] Unidentified Flying Object, aliens, the mother ship, ET, you get the drift.

nations has there been a worldwide consensus on anything? It would be sweet, but I remain skeptical.

Unless, of course, the Men in Black have visited me too.

Who's to say?

March 21ST, 2014 – 8 Hour Shift

Did I ever tell you the story of John Major, the Alien expert of Randall Rd?" Jon asked me during a particularly slow shift.

"You did not," I said. "Please, regale me with the story of John Major."

"You bet!" he shifted and leaned in for dramatic effect. "John is an interesting sort. He used to call constantly and report that aliens were reading his thoughts. He could hear them whispering in his head at all times. According to the deputies that dealt with this man, he would wear tin-foil helmets in an effort to block their alien signals."

Of course, this description is not in any official report. I checked.

"John would call regularly and report these attacks by aliens. One deputy, Deputy Arnoldson, convinced this individual that the aliens had sensitive sensors. One effective way to combat the signals would be to line his property with metal spoons angled upwards. John went to the thrift shop, purchased the metal spoons, which acted as mini-satellite dishes, and blocked the signals from the aliens."

"Yeah? How'd that work out for him?" I asked.

"Clearly, it worked since you've never heard from the man reporting alien signals," he spun around towards his computers.

"Did that man get a job at the 911 dispatch center to make my life more fulfilled?" I asked.

"What?" Jon said.

"John, the guy with the alien signals... is Jon sitting across me, no longer getting alien signals because we're in a bunker... are you picking up what I'm putting down?"

At least I think I'm funny.

"Ha. Maybe," Jon said. No genuine chuckle. "Naw, I'm a Jonathan, and you know my last name isn't Major."

"I don't know how deep this cover-up goes," I turned to my computers.

"Seriously though, the spoons are still there. Drive by 714 Randall Rd sometime and check it out. You can see them lining the yard from the road."

I did, and you can.

November 19TH, 2015 – 12 Hour Shift

My Deputies run the gamut regarding their belief in the supernatural. Some believe in Big Foot, and several have personal stories of encounters, all conveniently undocumented and unwitnessed. Some believe openly in aliens but that we have not yet made contact. Some think the whole notion is malarkey.

It is interesting to see these people review their different theories, all embedded with their personal experiences. In this line of work, many things go unexplained. Strange and crazy things happen, which defy any rational explanation.

One example was a thief who would have otherwise been set free, except the deputy reportedly noticed that his aura was the wrong color.

We sat in the center just after midnight on a remarkably peaceful night. I had made some burgers for a few of the guys on shift, including Deputy LeBraun.

"So, you can see auras?" I asked, ever inquisitive.

"Yes," LeBraun answered.

I was slightly shocked that someone in his position would admit to such a thing.

"They shift for different reasons, one of which is deceit," he explained.

"Yeah, I'm going to need more than that," I said.

"For instance, if a person has a bright yellow aura at rest and they lie, it may shift to a red color. Their face remains motionless, and nothing changes except the color around them."

Initially, I'd think that LeBraun was messing with me, but it's not his nature to kid around. He's a pretty level-headed, straightforward kind of guy. I don't even think I have ever heard him laugh.

"Obviously, this would not be admissible in court, so how do you use it to your advantage?" I genuinely want to know more.

"Well, last week, when I arrested that guy for the Shell Station robbery, I had difficulty proving it. He was wearing a full ski mask in the video and different clothing when we located him, and we couldn't find the gun. So the only reason we had enough to detain him was that the vehicle he was driving matched the vehicle at the scene," LaBraun said.

Having the same make, model, and color of a vehicle in a crime is a good enough reason to do a Terry Stop[2]. It's even enough to detain someone for a certain length of time. Especially when it's a violent crime. However, we cannot make an arrest if we don't have sufficient evidence.

"I saw when I first pulled up that he had a blue aura," LaBraun said. "I questioned him hard about it, and that's when I noticed his aura had shifted to a near-black color. I knew he was lying. I just had to find the tangible evidence."

As the story goes, the deputy and the suspect had an intense stare-down, and magically his story changed. He first admitted to being at the Shell Station, then eventually the robbery. A confession is good enough for an arrest. Afterward, they got a search warrant for the vehicle and found the gun, change of clothes, and stolen money in a suitcase in the trunk.

Was this an act of the beyond? Or was it just the intuition of an experienced deputy?

I'm open to the former and enjoy the fun stories it creates.

"What color is my aura?" Jon asked sarcastically.

---

[2] Named for the landmark US Supreme Court case, Terry v. Ohio. An officer may briefly detain and pat down the outer clothing of an individual if there is reasonable suspicion. In certain states, they have further requirements to stop, but that's the gist.

"A bright and distinct pink," I replied on Deputy LeBraun's behalf.

"What are we talking about?" Deputy Majewski asked, walking in while stuffing his face with a burger.

"The unexplained phenomenon experienced by my deputies," I said. "Are you telling them my Big Foot story?" Majewski said.

"I'm sorry, what?" I nearly choked.

Deputy Majewski is arguably one of the most burly men on the force. This man grew up in the backwoods. He is an avid tracker, hunter, fisherman, all around badass. One of his regular duties with the Sheriff's Office is to catch poachers. This dude works the wilderness, essentially alone. He reminds me of Paul Bunyan.

"When I was a young man, I had a date with my lady friend. I drove into the woods off the highway in my old extended-cab truck. We were in the back of the cab doing what young kids do in the middle of the woods. Suddenly, the entire truck was lifted and shook from the bed of the truck," Majewski motioned with his hands. "The whole damn thing had to be up in the air by about four or five feet."

"I was able to throw on some clothes quickly and get out of the vehicle," Majewski continued. "I armed myself with a 9mm and was ready for battle. By the time I got out, the suspect was nowhere to be found." He took another bite of his burger and swallowed. "The creature was able to rip the bed off its frame costing over a thousand dollars in damage. It wouldn't even drive right on the way home. Bed rattled the whole time."

"Ok, but how do you know this was Big Foot?" I ask.

"When I got the truck to the repair shop the next day, all this brown fur was lodged into the tailgate's cracks. The lady I was with said that while I was getting dressed, she saw what looked like a bear out the back window."

As the story goes, he attempted to recreate the scene with a couple of his friends, and no one, even working as a team, could recreate the lift or damage caused by the Big Foot.

Years after that, Majewski had another run-in that was less compelling. He was out pheasant hunting, and his dogs chased a Big Foot-like creature through the same woods. He did not get a good look at it then either, yet he remains 100% sure that Big Foot exists and believes it is still around today.

"I believe in Big Foot," Jon said.

"Oh yeah?" I asked, surprised by how quiet he had been through these stories.

"Yeah, its name is Pam, and it will relieve you at 0700 hours."

June 5TH, 2017 – 12 Hour Shift

Not all strange occurrences turn out to have such a grandiose plotline. One night, we got a report of an elderly female, home alone, who reported hearing glass breaking. She was confident someone was in the house.

These types of calls often trigger this dispatcher's head because of the famous "Ruth" call. I stayed on the phone with her to give constant updates to the officer who was driving to the scene. After clearing the scene and finally labeling it as a "false alarm," I wondered what occurred.

"False alarm," I said after hanging up with Bernice, the elderly RP.

"That's good. I'm glad she's alright," Megan said, also concerned for the RP's well-being. Megan watched the call. "We'll have to read that report once he's done writing it."

Not all officers are willing to update us on the outcomes of calls. They are under no official obligation to tell us anything, and generally speaking, because we are sat out in the county, we have a closer working relationship with the deputies than we do with the city cops that we serve. In these cases, we have to wait to read the report after the fact. About an hour later, I saw that his report had been submitted.

"Oh! The report for that broken window false alarm has been posted," I said to Megan.

"Awesome. Read it out loud."

"I arrived on scene at a two-story home; dispatch told me the RP was in an upstairs bedroom. I immediately scanned the front of the home and up and down the block in both directions. No vehicles were on the streets or visible vehicles in any surrounding driveways. I shined my main light onto the front yard and began my search of the house. There was no sign of entry at the front of the house and no signs of broken glass anywhere to be found. I then searched the east side of the residence. There was only one window, and it was intact. I returned to the front of the house and proceeded to the west side of the residence. Upon surveying the windows on the west side, I determined that no entry had been attempted, and there were no signs of broken glass. I moved to the backside of the residence and instantly saw the broken glass. It was located about ten feet away from the backdoor. I scanned the backyard for someone, and it was then I located the subject."

"The subject? You said he cleared the call as a false alarm," Megan interrupted.

"He was about one foot tall, grey shirt, black gloves, and a mask on his face. He squeaked as he fled the scene. I opted not to pursue the suspect, as I was uncertain of the level of crime at this point. Upon further inspection of the broken glass, I determined the source was a glass bottle from the recycling bin. It was clear to me that the assailant was, in fact, a raccoon and that raccoon was obviously a member of Al Qaeda, the middle-east based terrorist group sent to shatter Americans' feeling of safety and security. I checked to see if I could see where the suspect fled, but the trail had gone cold. I contacted the resident and explained my findings. She was oddly relieved, even though I told her the suspect had fled and was still at large."

"Oh, my god. That is amazing," Megan said.

We were both laughing hard at this point. "I can't believe he actually wrote that in the official report.

I am sure this type of reporting is wildly out of protocol and could potentially result in some sort of disciplinary action. Although I thought it was hilarious, apparently, so did the officer.

"We have to find the joy in the little things, I guess."

August 12TH, 2013 – 8 Hour Shift

We have to report all flying incidents to the the Federal Aviation Administration also known as the FAA. Flying remains one of the safest modes of transport per capita, but the tiny fleets of airplanes flown by either amateurs or private pilots still tend to crash more often than folks realize. What I found most shocking as a dispatcher is how common plane crashes are. I've personally taken about one call per year about a plane crash.

My first plane crash was a Cessna, and it had only the pilot onboard.

"Well, here we go," Terrance uttered as the 911 lines lit up.

When all call-takers are busy with phone calls, there is an audible tone throughout the room to let us know there are more 911 calls than call-takers. We call it "the gonger."

High-visibility incidents along the highway or in a public setting tend to inundate the 911 Center. As a result, we know instantaneously when something significant has happened.

This plane had crash-landed on a golf course near the town center. A lot of people witnessed it, and every single person called 911. Thankfully, filtering through the calls is more manageable after we get all the pertinent information and the appropriate response en route.

"Is this about the plane that crashed at the golf course?"

"Were you involved at all?"

"Yep. We've had a ton of calls about this already. Thank you."

If you call 911 about a crash on the freeway or some other incident and the 911 call-taker is very short with you—I promise, it is not their intent to be rude, they are slammed. If you are not directly involved and we already have the information we need about the incident, we no longer require every single testimony. If you genuinely want to recount events, stick around, be patient, and get interviewed by a police officer making the official report.

I never found out what caused that first crash; ultimately, it does not matter. The pilot was dead on impact.

"Did someone already call the FAA?" Mike The Dick, and supervisor, asked the room.[3]

"Yeah, we did with all our free time," Terrance whispered in my earshot.

"Right, I wonder how many calls he picked up during that," I muttered.

"I don't have to wonder. I looked over at him several times, hoping he would get the hint that we were all getting our asses handed to us," Terrance said.

"You always give him too much credit," I laughed.

"Hello? Did someone notify the FAA?" He isn't called Mike The Dick for nothing.

The room stayed silent for another minute. I was too new at this point to add my two cents yet. Otherwise, I'm sure I would have offered a more sarcastic quip. Especially when he stood up to glare at us. I just shook my head at him when we made eye contact.

---

[3] Yep, that's his first, middle, and last name. Well, for the purpose of this book, it is.

"I guess I'll take care of it then," Mike The Dick said.

"What a martyr," I whispered.

"He is my literal hero. I hope to grow up just like him," Terrance said.

The phones rang again.

The stragglers.

My other favorite type of caller.

"Hey did you know a plane crashed on the golf course?" asked the RP.

"Is this another one? Or the same one that crashed about thirty minutes ago? The police, medics, and fire trucks are on the scene for that call," I said.

"Yeah, I just wanted to make sure you knew."

"Yep. That's how the police, medics, and fire trucks arrived."

July 3RD, 2014 –12:38 – 8 Hour Shift

My second plane crash was particularly tragic. The first call came from an elderly female who thought she saw a UFO. The 2nd and 3rd callers lived across the way from the hill and were reporting some sort of wreck—with pieces of said wreck all over the hillside.

The first units on the scene realized right away that it was, in fact, a plane crash. It impacted into the side of a large wooded, hilly area. They also realized they would have to upgrade it into a technical rescue since there was no way up the hill with a fire truck or ambulance. [4] The initial crew

119

started an on-foot approach to attempt to locate any survivors.

"It will take them a while to get up that hill on foot. That's right by my grandpa's house. That hill is steep," said Sheila, who was working the Fire radio on this shift.

"Do you need any assistance at all? I can ask Audrey if I can take over your radio so you can set up a tac channel and focus solely on this," I said.

"Yes, that would be great. I have a feeling this will take a while," Sheila said.

I knew it was severe. Sheila is a proud dispatcher who does not like giving up her workload. She thinks she can do everything and doesn't often ask for assistance. Even offering to take her radio could be seen as me thinking she was weak.

According to her, of course.

When I first started dispatching, I was definitely like that too. I did not want to appear like I couldn't handle the job. However, through my CISM training, I learned this mentality is prevalent among all first responders. It's commonly referred to as Hero Syndrome or Savior Complex—someone who always strives to be the hero of the situation. No matter the odds, they want to be the ones who save the day. It's churlish, and the older we get in the dispatch center, the more we realize that heroism comes from all of the parts working together, assisting each other as one cohesive team.

---

[4] This is much larger response, including specialized equipment based on the training etc.

I firmly believe that Hero Syndrome employees stem from poor management—another unfortunate common thread in dispatch centers.[5]

I digress.

The first of the fire units finally made it to a piece of the tail. They gave dispatch the numbers off the airplane, and with that information, we were able to get the flight plan and find out who was on board.

"The pilot was a man in his mid-60s; on board was his wife," Sheila broadcasted to the units on her tac channel.

"Oh, that's sad," I said.

Sheila stepped on her pedal, "As well as their two grandchildren."

"Oh fuck," my heart sank.

According to the reports of the crew on scene, they never actually recovered a body, only parts.

"A war-like level of destruction," stated one of the firefighters dispatched to the scene.

This call affected all of the responders. The CISM team created a debriefing immediately. A defusing, due to the nature of the scene, followed it.

July 13TH, 2015 – 8 Hour Shift

"Oh my god, not again," I said, pushing out tones to the fire department. "Medic 15, Medic 18, Engine 15, respond to the

---

[5] See, Mike The Dick. No, really guys, he's the worst.

18 hundred block of Highway One for a report of a downed aircraft, reports of an explosion, and a ball of fire."

"Uh, dispatch, let's get a few more engines started if a ball of fire was reported." I guess. Engine 15 didn't want to be the only one at the party.

"Copy that."

As I started a couple more engines, Melanie, one of the newer call-takers, stopped by my desk. "One of my callers said they captured it on their dash cam, and they're going to put it up on Twitter. They said that the fireball was massive."

"Do they think everyone's dead then?" I asked, not sure if I really wanted the answer yet.

"When I asked about survivors, he said, and I quote, *there's no way anyone could walk away from that one.*"

"Yikes. You off to break?" Melanie nodded. "Ok, if you find the footage, text it to me. I want to see it."

"Will do."[6]

Melanie walked away, aggressively swiping at her phone.

I continued to work the scene, showing my units arriving in CAD, making notifications, and ensuring that someone notified the FAA. I didn't get up, holler across the room, and stare at people like some dicks. Instead, I sent everyone a message, and someone rogered up to make the call.

"Engine 18 to dispatch."

"Go ahead, Engine 18."

"Yeah, uh, we have no victims here. Any other incoming units can stand down."

I must have misheard.

---

[6] I told you, we're sick.

After double-checking Engine 18 was actually at the plane crash and finding they were, "Engine 18 confirming, there are *zero* victims at the plane crash?"

"Uh, that's correct dispatch. Zero victims."

I was so confused.

My phone buzzed.

Melanie sent me a text. It was a link to a Twitter post. The dash-cam footage was visually stunning. As the plane approached the ground, it struck a series of powerlines, causing a large explosion with flames shooting fifty feet into the air. The small ATEC aircraft hit the ground with its wheels already prepped for landing, bounced, and rolled into two vehicles on the ground. You could hear the voices of the videographer and friends in the background.

"Oh my god! That was a huge explosion!"

"They're dead, they're dead! No way anyone survived that!"

I heard through the grapevine that heavy traffic made the scene immensely difficult to access. The crash was in the middle of the highway at a major intersection of a perpendicular road. By the time the firefighters arrived, the flames had dispersed, and no visible fires were in the area. Perplexed, they initially thought they were at the wrong intersection.

Remarkably, not a single person was injured.

7

That Is A Very Permanent Solution To A Temporary Problem

Dispatch: 911, where is your emergency?

Male Caller: I believe I may be having a heart attack.

Dispatch: Ok, and how long has this been going on for?

Male Caller: I've been experiencing it on and off for several hours, but now it's increasing to the point where I think I need to go to the hospital.

Dispatch: Ok, have you been prescribed any nitroglycerin?

Male Caller: No, sir. Do you know how long it's going to take for them to get here?

Dispatch: I don't have an ETA for you, unfortunately, but I can stay on the phone until they arrive if you'd like.

Male Caller: No. I'll be fine. Don't worry about me. I can manage until they get here.

Dispatch: Are you sure? I don't mind waiting on the phone and keeping you company.

Male Caller: Oh, hush. I will be fine! I'm sure. You have more important things to do.

Dispatch: Ok, just call me back if anything changes before they arrive, ok?

Male Caller: Of course.

radio traffic

Medic Unit: Uh… Dispatch, we're going to need law to respond.

Dispatch: Ok, can you advise for what?

Medic Unit: The patient has a bullet wound to the back of the head. He's DOA.

Confused?

I sure was.

The deputy dispatched to the scene was equally perplexed. He called me right away to ask what I heard. I told him the conversation exactly. It was a run-of-the-mill chest pain call. I told him I offered to stay on the line because he sounded scared. I heard no one else in the background, and he made no mention of any head pain.

This was my first *trick suicide* call.

Suicides are most common amongst the elderly, more so than any other demographic. There are a lot of reasons for this. They are lonely, all of their friends and family have passed on, chronic pain from diseases and/or advanced stages of cancer, and depression are among the top reasons.

Every suicide is slightly different, but many of them have specific patterns. Elderly people who have made up their minds that they are going to die will generally call 911 to ensure that first responders find their bodies before the families do. In their minds, death is a routine thing for us; therefore, we will be better equipped to handle the trauma of a dead body.

Generally, I find that most callers, who have decided to die, will have a familiar calm demeanor, and they simply say, "I am at such and such address; I am going to be shooting myself. Come and find the body, please."

The end.

It is short, sweet, and direct. There is no discussion. Their minds have been made up, and they do not want to be talked out of it.

The transcript above was reminiscent of this type of call, except instead, he decided to feign a heart attack to avoid further questioning about a suicide plan and still get the responders there promptly.

This was a calculated suicide.

"What exactly did you hear on the line?" the deputy asked, probing me for more information.

"Nothing. He was a sweet old man. As I said before, he sounded a little scared, but he declined when I offered to stay on the line. He asked for an ETA, but that's normal too for people."

"You didn't hear anyone in the background?"

"No. Why?" My head swirling with the possibility that I had missed some crucial detail. I started doubting what I heard. I told the deputy I would play back the call on my recorder and let him know if I heard anything different.

The call was as I remembered.

The medic reported a bullet wound to the *back of the head*. The gun was a riffle, making it ostensibly abnormal for the RP to hold a rifle behind his head and shoot.

After the deputies got on the scene, it was determined that the *back of the head* to a medic meant the entrance wound was behind his right ear on the *side* of his head. The RP had put the shotgun on the ground, pointing upwards, and then laid his head on the end of the barrel before pulling the trigger.

I was pretty shaken up by this call for a while. I replayed it repeatedly in my head, wondering what I could have done or said differently to save him.

"It's not your job to save them," Jon said.

"I mean, it kind of is."

"Not at all. We are not trained to counsel these people. That's why we have a suicide hotline to transfer them to people trained in psychology and therapy." Jon had a point.

"If it's our job to connect suicidal folk with therapists, then saving them by making the connection?" I was going to win this argument.

"By that extension, isn't Alexander Graham Bell, the creator of phones, the true hero? After all, we can only transfer callers because of his invention."

I was not going to win this argument.

"Fine." I sat in my defeat.

"We are nothing more than glorified repeater towers. We push the buttons and click the things." Jon has such a fresh and humbled outlook on everything.

"You keep me grounded, Jon, and I appreciate you."

June 17TH, 2015 – 8 Hour Shift

"I need you to stay over this morning. Melanie called in sick," Mike The Dick grunted.

"No, I can't. I've already gotten three mandatory overtime shifts this week, and I have to take my son to school this morning," I said. "I don't have anyone else. Otherwise, I would stay," I said, trying to appeal to his better nature.

"Well, there's nobody else, and everyone's at three mandos this week." He said.

"I'm sorry, but I really can't. Are you able to maybe call someone to come in?" I said.

"No one ever answers their phone when I call," he walked away. "Gee, I wonder why," I said under my breath.

Thankfully, Megan offered to stay over. It would be her fourth time this week. Poor lady. I asked if I could grab her some food or coffee.

"A coffee would be nice. Thank you," Megan sighed.

"Thank you for staying. My son's mother is out of town this week. Otherwise, I would have offered to stay."

"No, I get it. I don't have anything going on this morning other than sleeping, and this way, they can't get me on my days off," Megan said. She looked for the silver linings.

I left to eat lunch. I brought it from home and ate as fast as possible so I could still run to the 24-hour coffee stand up the road for Megan. Cream and a Splenda.

We all knew each other's coffee orders. It's nearly a currency in the Comm Center. Some people have fancy drinks that cost $17, and you know not to offer them unless you feel extra generous. While others, like myself, prefer it black.

When I got back to my desk, I handed Megan her coffee. She thanked me but looked even more upset.

"Uh oh, what happened?" I asked, not sure I wanted to hear the answer.

"Right when you left, I got a guy with two shotgun holes to the chest."

"Ouch. Where at?"

"In his chest," Megan said.

I laughed, trying not to be so overt, "No, I mean where, as in who's jurisdiction?"

"Oh. County. Gosh, I really do need this coffee if I'm going to make it through this."

"Did they catch the shooter?"

"As a matter of speaking, I guess so."

Wow. She is exhausted.

"Uh, what does *that* mean?" I asked.

"It was a suicide."

"Oh. I thought I heard the victim had two gunshot wounds to the chest."

"Yep. You heard right." Megan took a sip of her coffee and looked back at her screen.

"How does that work?" I was very puzzled.

The man had somehow managed to shoot himself in the chest with a rifle, not die, and then shoot himself a second time. It is incredible to me that one could inflict such horrible pain on oneself and then have the ability to fire again to finish the job.

This peculiar case required extra investigation before ultimately ruling it a suicide. It was a strange weapon of choice for suicide, and the second shot is still suspicious.

"I have more suicides under my belt than any other dispatcher in this Comm Center," I complained.

"It is just the luck of the draw. We each tend to have our *specialties*. I have the most CPR in progress calls," Pam said, trying to be consoling.

I think.

"Yeah, and you have the most additional kills while doing CPR in the Comm Center," Jon interjected.

"Oh yeah? How do you manage that?" I asked.

"That only happened twice," Pam laughed. "In both cases, an old lady found her husband unconscious. So I started coaching CPR, and boom—her heart gave out, and she collapsed over dead right on the husband."

"That happened twice?" I said, in shock.

"Yeah."

"Why do I find that kind of sweet? I mean, at least they died together." I plugged in for my shift. "What's *your* specialty, Jon?"

"He has the record for most mistakes on a call," Pam said.

"Oooh, ouch," I laughed.

I volunteered for extra training around suicide calls because of the frequency I received them. However, as a 911 dispatcher, it is neither my duty nor my responsibility to become a grief counselor. I am not here to talk anyone off a ledge or ensure that everything will be ok.

I cannot do either of those things.

My job is to gather as much information about the incident as I can and to ensure that the suicidal subject is not going to be a threat to my responders. Beyond that, I can do my best to keep them talking or be a supportive ear for them to vent to. Ultimately what happens to them is not my fault.

A crucial piece of training for 911 dispatchers is to remember to be direct.

We will not make someone suicidal by asking bluntly, "Are you thinking about committing suicide?" If the RP is indecisive about details, generally, they are less likely to be an immediate threat to themselves. They likely have things to get off their chest, are in a state of crisis, and are crying out for help. The ones with means and a specific plan will be the imminent threat. It is not a crime to commit suicide, and I try to respect each person's individual right to choose.

Some suicides are downright selfish.

"Charlie 17, Charlie 20 for a suspicious call," I broadcasted.

"Go ahead."

"Contact RP at the middle school on Morgan Lane regarding what they believe to be a Halloween decoration in the tree on the playground."

"Copy, show us en route."

"A Halloween decoration in May?" Jon said, eavesdropping.

"Yeah, I have no idea." I watched as the units arrived on the scene.

"Charlie 20 to Dispatch."

"Go ahead, Charlie 20."

"Roll fire this way. Tell them they'll likely need a ladder."

"What do we have?"

"We got a guy who hanged himself. He's pretty far up. I'd estimate 25-30 feet."

I messaged the fire dispatcher to start some units. It was initially investigated as a murder, but I heard later that it was finally ruled a suicide. He made no call to 911. He made no attempt to save himself that could be determined. Instead, he went to a public place. At an elementary school, during the school week, he climbed high up into a tree and hung himself. It was not immediately clear whether this was a political statement or whether he wanted his body discovered so that no one would miss it.

To commit such a public display in front of children is obscene, selfish, inconsiderate, and unconscionable. I have zero respect or sympathy for the people who commit these types of suicides.

There are some suicidal subjects whom I could consider to be "accidentally" selfish.

One afternoon, a man who drove eighty miles from his home parked his vehicle in a secluded yet beautiful wooded area and shot himself in the head. He was still in his vehicle, and he ensured he was in a semi-private area.

His remains were not discovered until nearly two months later.

The person that found him was so shaken up by the incident we had to send an additional ambulance to deal with the catatonic RP.

In contrast to the man who hanged himself in the tree at the playground, this subject tried to not be discovered. Hence, *they are accidentally* selfish. Nevertheless, he still inflicted horror on a complete stranger. That's not even touching on the pain, suffering, and unanswered questions left on the family and friends of the departed.

I handle suicidal subjects on a near-daily basis. After a while, I really started to respect the "come find my body" tactics. It is respectful of the people who are going to find the body. The aid crew knows what they will encounter before they arrive; honestly, the family will not be the first to discover the body.

If you are feeling suicidal, there are resources out there for you.

You can call the **National Suicidal Prevention Lifeline at 1-800-273-8255**. They also have specific resources for Veterans. **Lines for Life: Military Hotline at 1-888-457-4838.** One of my favorite organizations is the **Trevor Project for LGBTQ individuals at 1-866-488-7386**. These people have a LOT more emotional training and support than I or any 911 Dispatcher can offer.

April 17TH, 2019 – 12 Hour Shift

"You should ask Kyle over there for some advice," I overheard Jon saying to Devon, a new call-taker.

"I thought his name was Jackson?" Devon said.

"Hey, Kyle! You should come over here and talk to Devon here. He just had his first suicidal subject and needs some coaching."

Aww, Jon believes in me.

Or was this a setup?

"What's going on?" I asked.

"Devon here asked me how to best deal with a suicidal caller. Apparently, his last call didn't go great, and he's afraid he might have pushed someone over the edge," Jon said.

Devon still had life and joy in his eyes.

God, I love a newbie.

"Gotcha. Well, what happened?" I asked.

"Well, I was talking to this woman. She told me she was having a bad day and wanted to go to the hospital, but she wouldn't give me any sort of complaint. I ruled out all medical possibilities. She started crying, and I told her I wanted to help her, but I couldn't if she couldn't tell me what was wrong."

I already knew where this was going, but I let him continue.

"I told her that I couldn't put in a call if I didn't know what was wrong. So anyway, she yells at me, says she will kill herself, and hangs up."

I wanted to giggle. Instead bottled it up and decided to create a teachable moment while mentoring this kid.

"Did you ask if she wanted to commit suicide?" I asked.

"No," Devon said.

"Why not?"

"I don't know. I guess I figured she would have told me."

134

Devon was using his critical thinking skills, even if it was wrong.

"Sometimes it's hard for people with suicidal ideation to admit it to a stranger. They're afraid of the idea and the word. This is how they reach out, and they don't know what to do. They're looking to us for assistance, and we can't be afraid of the questions."

Damn.

I even surprised myself with how grownup I've become.

"That makes sense," Devon said.

"You will save yourself a lot of time and anguish if you knock it out right away," I said. "After you've ruled out medical reasons for the desire to go to a hospital, you can simply ask, *Are you thinking about committing suicide*? It's direct, and the question may shock them, but they'll feel more comfortable with you if you knock that barrier down for them."

"I guess I was afraid of asking. But you're right. We need to take charge."

He's going to be ok.

I started to walk away.

"But wait, I thought your name was Jackson?"

I smiled.

One of my favorite intervention techniques was creating "Kyle."

In my work, we deal with people in our community. Many strange individuals that you may run into in real life. I've already discussed that sometimes, we know the people calling. Thus, as a rule of thumb, I never use my real name at work.[1]

Management knows this. They understand and support those of us who wish to maintain anonymity on this side of the phone.

Kyle was created to add a personal touch to assist suicidal callers who just need someone to talk to or a reason to live.

"No one cares if I live or die."

"Well, my name is Kyle, and I care. You've called me, and I'm now involved, so please help Kyle help you."

It sounds corny, but it helps me connect with people I would not usually have a connection with.

November 12TH, 2020 – 12 Hour Shift

Mark called 911. He was despondent and unhappy with life.

"Are you considering suicide Mark?" I asked bluntly.

"To be honest, yes," he said.

Mark told me he was in his car but did not want to share where he was. He let me know that he was armed with a loaded handgun and was thinking about ending it all.

I don't know, Mark.

I don't know his life.

I can't sit there and assure him I know exactly what he is going through. It won't be genuine if I try to connect in that manner. But, most importantly, Mark would notice.

Instead, I introduce myself as Kyle.

"Mark, I know I can't possibly understand your situation. We've never met. However, you called *me*. That was for a

---

[1] Or in a book, apparently.

reason. My name is Kyle, and I need you to help me help you. Tell me what's going on with you. I want to know."

Kyle made the connection instantly. He put the responsibility on Mark to not disappoint Kyle. Kyle flows with the call and gets Mark to open up while I simultaneously track his phone.

Mark had money, relationship, and a whole breed of issues. His problems were universally human. It's not that I, Jackson, cannot relate. The problem is that there is no point if I can't sound genuine.

Instead, I deploy empathy through the persona, Kyle.

"Wow, I can't imagine going through all of that. You said no one cares about you, Mark, but you called me. You involved me, and I care. Can you help me?" I asked.

Turning the tables on a suicidal caller is my specialty. Now he is responsible for me. Feeling out the situation is crucial. Each RP is going to be different.

Eventually, I found Mark. He never did confess his location. Keeping him on the phone talking, I located him via his cellphone ping. I used Kyle to get him to put down the gun and speak with the officers. It was a masterclass in patience for me.

Thankfully Kyle is good at his job.

February 2ND, 2020 – 12 Hour Shift

One Sunday afternoon, a woman called who was in a mental health crisis, especially considering she was suicidal. She was stressed over insufficient money to put gasoline in her vehicle and get food for her dog.

The RP was particularly tricky because she called on a business line, which does not allow us to track her GPS location while talking with her.

I attempted a similar technique used with Mark. Unfortunately, "Kyle cares" did not work. She was at her emotional limit with her dog, and adding Kyle to the mix did not help.

Switching gears, I focused on her dog. If she commits suicide, who will take care of her dog?

I got brutal.

The dog would be taken to the pound, and if it is older, which it was, the dog would be put down. The city doesn't want to waste resources on an unadoptable dog.

"There are no-kill shelters," she said.

"Maybe, but you won't be there to make the determination. You don't get to decide which shelter he goes to," I said.

Finally, she was calm enough to tell me where she was, and she agreed to talk to one of my friends, a cop. But unfortunately, not all of our officers are great at de-escalation techniques. The first officer on-scene spun her back up into a craze, and she locked herself inside her vehicle.

She felt "Kyle" had betrayed her. So, she called 911 again to yell at me, Kyle, for sending such a jerk. I had to apologize and ultimately send a more "trained" friend to talk to her.

The second officer was much more formidable at playing her *game*. He took his time and got her to comply with limited interventions. The second officer called me afterward to thank me for doing such a great job with her. A rare treat, I assure you. We agreed that not everyone could be as calm, smooth, and demure as Kyle.

Maybe one day, I'll grow up to be as smooth as Kyle.

December 9TH, 2021 – 8 Hour Shift

Tbe first time I ever spoke with Brenda, I really fell for it. Brenda sold me a story of how she had gotten her hands on a gun. She was going to drive to the end of the boatyard and end it all. She told me about Brad. Brad had left her for a younger woman, and now her life was over. Brenda speaks with passion and concern. She may even believe the stories she makes up in her head.

Brenda is a local transient. She enjoys being liquored up, romanticizing a life she never had, and acting out drama on the streets of our fair city. Brenda is not suicidal. Brenda is an alcoholic and probably schizophrenic. However, when Brenda calls 911 and tells me she has a gun and plans to end her life, I must take that as seriously as any other call.

Brenda, and the people like her, make our job even more difficult. When you have these callers, it is tough to stay compassionate and empathetic towards people in severe crises. It's the boy who cried wolf over and over again.

We have other people who are not schizophrenic or alcoholics who call routinely to report that they are suicidal when they are not. I am sure other issues are happening, but they mostly tie up our resources for naught. These "attention-seekers," as I call them, can be a real burden on our emergency services, and they do sometimes hinder our responses to actual emergencies.

As 911 dispatchers, we often are allowed to go on ride-alongs with our officers. One night, I was riding with one of the city officers, Danko, and we got a report of a woman downtown crying in the middle of the roadway. She was reportedly having a hard time with a recent break-up.

"That'll be Brenda," Danko said.

"Yeah?" I asked.

"Yep. I wonder which imaginary husband left her this week," he said.

We get on the scene of an intoxicated woman who appears to be in her mid-50s. As I recall, she was only 43. Brenda walks up casually to the officer and me.

She knows the routine.

"Oh, Officer! Officer! I'm so glad you came," she speaks like an actor in an old black and white movie, very Blanche Deveraux,[2] "I lost my husband Ralph last year in the war. I'm just torn to pieces."

"Oh yeah? Which war was this?" asked the officer halfheartedly.

"The war! The war that's going on for years! I'm just torn to pieces!" the charade continued.

"Ok, and why are you grieving publicly in the middle of the roadway?" Danko asked.

"Well, I just cannot be alone tonight," she explained.

---

[2] Didn't think I could squeeze in a Golden Girls reference, did you?

140

"That's fine, but can you grieve somewhere that isn't in the middle of the roadway? You are impeding traffic, people are concerned for your safety, and they keep calling 911," Danko said.

"I am… just… soo… saa…." She trailed off into a puddle of her own tears.

"Why don't you come with me to the shelter?" Danko guided her to the downstairs of the Veterans Center, where they host a homeless shelter during the colder winter months.

Brenda decided to escalate her crisis. The officer felt it was better left to the mental health professionals at this point, so he called the crisis line for her.

We stood there as she poured her heart out about her life to the poor sap at the crisis line. It was interesting to hear her ramble on about her belated Ralph when she cried to me about her former husband Jeffrey just two nights before. I believe it was Peter before that, and of course, there was her first husband, Brad.

Suicidal callers do not affect me the way they do other people. Of course, I feel sorry for the loved ones that they have left behind. But I don't judge them, and I don't see them as being selfish or crazy. Suicidal subjects are living in survival mode. They have to take one day at a time and fight every moment to survive. Their obstacles may be financial, mental, physical, emotional, or a combination.

I think each of us has felt survival mode at some point; for many of us, it is a temporary state of being. We work through the situation, and maybe it lasts a day or two, perhaps a week, or even a tough month.

We get through it.

When you live in survival mode for years, the dynamic changes. Everyone's story is different. At the end of the day, it all boils down to the breaking point.

An elderly person tired of the pain of cancer decides suicide will end the physical pain. A transgender person living daily feeling "incorrect" or "broken" decides suicide because they feel they do not have a place in society. A wife of an abusive husband with no work or life experience outside the abusive home decides suicide is her only way out. Unfortunately, not everyone has the strength, opportunity, or education to escape their situation.

After many years on this job, I can tell you that a LOT of people live in survival mode.

Just be kind to each other. You don't know what other people's struggles are.

Let's all care like Kyle.

8

If Life Is A Highway, I Want To Ride It Until About 9pm And Then Get A Good Night's Rest

Dispatch: 911, where is your emergency?

Female Caller: Yes, I'm on highway one, where it meets highway two.

Dispatch: Ok, what is going on there?

Female Caller: I see a man on the side of the road, and he is acting very strangely.

Dispatch: Ok, what is he doing?

Female Caller: Well, he is walking back and forth and waving an inappropriate thing at the truck drivers as they go by.

Dispatch: What is this inappropriate thing he has?

Female Caller: Uhm…. A dildo.

A few minutes later, the deputy got on the scene to find a white male in his 40s walking on the side of the road, carrying a seven-inch dildo in his right hand.

"What have you got there?" Deputy Marks asked the man.

"Um, a toy."

"Ok, we got complaints of you waving it around at people. So what's going on tonight?"

The deputy stated in his official report that the subject was attempting to flag truckers down. The deputy advised the subject to find a more conventional means of attracting a mate.

December 29TH, 2018 – 12 Hour Shift

Drugs and alcohol combined with driving a vehicle is a lethal combination. Unfortunately, it kills innocent people in other vehicles more often than the intoxicated driver during a DUI collision. Thankfully, there is a lot of public education about this in the world. I will not spend much time on all of their statistics and horrible death stories.

Drinking and driving is both illegal and stupid.

Getting high and driving is both illegal and stupid.

Depending on their effects, prescription medications and driving may be a DUI. Please follow the instructions on the medication bottles. If you have any doubts, do not drive.

"Hey guys, there are some extra training modules in the online portal if you're interested," said Matt, the newly promoted supervisor who was trying too hard.

"Are they required?" I asked.

"No. But there are some excellent resources in there, and I just thought I'd let you know if you wanted to be an overachiever."

"Oh, Matt. No. I know you're new to this position, but you know me. I am not an overachiever. I like to achieve. Not over. Not under."

"I can attest to that. You're a solid B+ person," Jon said from behind me.

"Awww, that might be the nicest thing you have ever said to me," I said.

A weird squeak went off in my headset. I turned to my computer. A city officer signed in for duty from his home and was heading southbound on the main highway into the office.

144

He had barely taken two sips of his coffee when a dark blue 1989 Lincoln Continental sped passed his patrol car, nearly taking off his driver's side mirror.

The only transmission I got over the radio was, "I am in pursuit of one."

It was on.

"Dark blue older model Ford Lincoln four-door, occupied times two."

Within seconds, all the officers in the area were en route to assist. The vehicle was still traveling southbound with extreme lane travel and near collisions. The vehicle's speeds were in excess of seventy miles per hour.

"We are now heading eastbound on Protection Avenue."

This was good luck for the pursuing officer. Protection Avenue was a dead end. It leads into a subdivision with only three or four side streets attached to it. Most of the homes are vacation rentals with very few permanent residents.

"Charlie 17, I'm going to have you sit at the end of Protection Avenue at the highway to block the only way in or out," I instructed.

"Copy that."

"Charlie 19, I'll head into the subdivision to check the gate."

"Copy Charlie 19."

"Charlie 8, still behind the vehicle. Speeds decreased to approximately 35 miles per hour and continued lane travel. Attempting PIT," Charlie 8 said. "PIT failed. My patrol car was damaged, and the vehicle sped up. I lost sight." [1] A piece

---

[1] A PIT maneuver is a tactical driving technique used by law enforcement.

145

of the Lincoln got wedged into the passenger-side-front-wheel of the patrol car and damaged the wheel well.

"What have you got going on over there?" Matt asked from the supervisor's desk.

"A pursuit. The suspect vehicle damaged a patrol car so badly that it could not follow. As a result, the officer lost sight of the suspect vehicle. I got another patrol unit that was able to catch up to the damaged unit and attempted to take over the pursuit. However, the new unit searched to the end of the street, and the suspect vehicle disappeared," I said.

Additional units got into the sub-division to assist in the search of the Lincoln. Unfortunately, after about fifteen minutes and with five officers searching, including the one at the end of Protection Avenue, they could not locate the Lincoln.

"Protection Avenue has no way out; the side streets are also dead-ends. Those dead ends back into heavy-forested areas with no trails and a creek. At the other end, Protection Avenue goes to the highway and ends," Matt says. He's good at stating the obvious. "At the other end was only… the cliff."

"Charlie 19, if you're done checking the subdivision, try the end of Protection by the turnaround to see if he continued past the field," I said.

The cliff at the end of Protection Avenue was steep and went down approximately 200 feet to the beach. It was rocky, full of trees and extensive root systems that jutted from the cliff's sides. From the end of the roadway, you must go through a field, up a small rocky terrain covered with tall, skinny trees, and then reach the cliff. I did not think it was likely that a vehicle could make it that way.

That was the moment Charlie 19 queued up the radio. "Oh yeah, we've got tire marks over here."

The Lincoln had continued forward at approximately fifty miles per hour into a small tree, then flipped over, launching both occupants from the vehicle and onto the cliffside. It was suspended upside down, hanging from a root system that was still ninty feet above the beach. The driver was under the vehicle by about ten feet but still up the cliff from the beach by eighty feet. The passenger was above the vehicle, on the cliffside in a tree, still seventy feet down the side of the cliff.

"Well, this is now a rescue mission," I said. I sent over a request to the fire dispatcher for the technical rescue. This would disappear from my screen and become a fire scene now. Incident command will now require a Fire Captain or higher to take over.

My part in this event was over. However, I still watched and completed a few tasks for the fire dispatcher.

The passenger of the vehicle was the easiest to recover. They lowered a Stokes Basket to the passenger and pulled him up. [2] On the other hand, the driver was still beneath the vehicle, which needed to be secured before the rescue team could go under to get him. Simultaneously, we attempted a beach access recovery with a fireboat. It was slow going.

"Can you call me a tow?" Jodi, the fire dispatcher, asked.

---

[2] Stokes Basket is a Metal wire or plastic stretcher on a system of pulleys widely used in Search and Rescue.

"Ok, you're a tow." It wasn't funny when I said it but overplayed jokes have their place.

That is a hill I will die on.

By the time the tow truck got his wench around the vehicle to secure it, the rescue team was able to retrieve the driver with the Stokes Basket.

Amazingly, both subjects survived the wreck. They arrested the driver after an evaluation in the hospital for DUI, attempting to elude, and reckless endangerment of his passenger. The driver was high on Methamphetamines. While the passenger was a hitchhiker, the driver picked up a few miles before the pursuit started. There was no reason why the driver decided to flee the police. According to the jail staff, after the driver had come down from his high, he had no memory of the incident at all.

March 27TH, 2015 – 12 Hour Shift

A lot of strange things happen on our roadways. Most of which I was blissfully ignorant of before I started working in dispatch.

The RP had little information and was reporting that on the side of Admiralty Way and the highway, there was a rolled-up carpet with something sticking out of the end.

I could hear the dread in the officer's voice when he told me he was en route.

"Did you just send Officer Jones to that carpet call?" Carrie asked. There was concern in her voice.

"Yeah. He was the only one I had available," I said.

"You should hold it and send it to someone else."

"Oh? Why?"

"Just get him off of that call first."

"Charlie 10, you can disregard that call," I broadcasted to Jones.

"I can continue in," Jones said.

"Charlie 12, show me clear of my call, and I'll back him."

"Copy." I turned to Carrie, "What's going on?"

Carrie is one of my more tenured colleagues. She told me a story from Officer Jones's early days in law enforcement. He found a female body wrapped up in a carpet that someone had tossed to the roadside. To this day, it's an unsolved murder.

"I don't know all the case details because he does not like to talk much about it," Carrie said.

"Well, now I feel horrible," I dispatched him to an eerily similar call. I am confident the experience of the previous carpet call was flashing in his mind.

Understandably, the officer took a long time to arrive on the scene. When he did, he advised us that he had located the carpet, and there was, in fact, something rolled up into it. There appeared to be bones sticking out one of the ends.

"Charlie 10, I'm going to standby for Charlie 12 before I go any further on this."

"Charlie 12, I'm only about 4 mins out."

"if this turns out to be another homicide, I'm officially the worst person on the planet," I said. My heart sank.

"You didn't know," Carrie said. "Furthermore, it's the nature of the job. The officers have to cope with the realities of the job and their experiences in the same ways we have to cope with ours."

It made me feel better.

Once both officers were on the scene, it was only a few minutes before the backing officer came on the radio, "Be advised, this is a deer that someone rolled up into the carpet. We have moved the carcass and carpet onto the side of the roadway. Please advise the roads department to pick up."

"Copy that," I sighed audibly. "What a relief."

We have no idea who did it or why they would roll a deer carcass up in a carpet. But we were quite glad it was a deer and not another human remains situation.

May 13TH, 2017 – 12 Hour Shift

Traffic-related incidents frequently include an extensive range of agencies responding to a single incident. A pursuit, for example, may start within a city's jurisdiction on a city street but then head out into the county jurisdiction, and therefore, the Sheriff's Office would take over. The vehicle may also go onto a highway or an interstate. In my state, that jurisdiction belongs to State Patrol. County jurisdictions have other jurisdictions that meet at different borders, sometimes including a different city's jurisdiction. For example, my county has seven counties that border it. In addition, not all cities share the same PSAP,[3] so several dispatch centers could be involved.

---

[3] AKA the 911 center.

Fast forward to a carjacking that occurred in a nearby city. The fleeing vehicle, a tan 2004 Chevrolet Malibu stolen by a male armed with a handgun. The original driver and owner of the vehicle was able to get out of the vehicle. The city police requested assistance from the county for that area as the pursuit started. The pursuit continued down the highway for several miles until it entered my jurisdiction.

Thankfully, the PSAP responsible for that area thought ahead enough to let us know this incident had occurred, so I was prepared. I positioned three deputies along the highway the suspect vehicle was barreling down.

They were prepared with spike strips.

It was a success.

All four tires were blown out. The suspect was taken into custody without incident.

I am fortunate enough to live in an area where the surrounding agencies all play well with each other. As I understand from conversations with other dispatchers on some of my blogs, this is not always the case. Sometimes, like at my center, the PSAPs share a linked CAD system so that if an incident requires the other's assistance, we can simply send the CFS to the next dispatcher center and instantaneously get the information. While other less fortunate dispatchers would have to call the neighboring PSAP and give all the information again, much the same as a 911 caller would. It can slow response times down.

Another type of jurisdictional difference is the sovereign nations of our Native Americans. Our Native Americans have separate police forces, laws, and court systems. Sometimes, they do share the same PSAPs for their police forces. For example, my particular agency has three Tribal Nations within its jurisdiction and dispatches for one of their police agencies.

"Tom 72 on traffic"

"Go ahead," I got my fingers ready.

"Show me out on Highway One. Mile marker 7. Black truck, obstructed plates, pulling a boat with no trailer."

"Copy." Confused, I repeated slowly, "Black truck towing a boat with no trailer. Highway One, mile marker 7."

He did not correct me.

This sparked some interest from a few other officers, and they went en route to back him. The next thing the officer requests is a check on fishing permits. This is also an odd request from an officer.

"Did he just ask for fishing permits?" Audrey was listening from the supervisor's desk.

"Yeah, I don't know. This officer is just barely out of the academy. Can we actually get a return for a fishing permit?"

"I don't think so, but honestly, I have no idea," she sat back down.

I start flipping through my quick reference manual, figuring out how to get a return for valid fishing permits. The other officer arrived on the scene to assist the first officer. The subsequent few transmissions are barely audible as the second officer is laughing through his words.

The entire thing was a complete misunderstanding. The "fishing permit" was not a fishing permit but a Tribal identification card. The truck was pulling a boat. The boat was on a trailer. The trailer had no *license plate*, which is not required on tribal lands. It took a while for the newbie officer to live that one down.

August 1ST, 2015 – 8 Hour Shift

An unfortunate side effect of traffic-related incidents is that most RP's drive by the incident and have limited knowledge of the whole scene. Alternatively, they just drove by the incident and have a slighted memory. One summer, we were plagued with a particularly interesting, reoccurring event that we could not catch in action.

Every Wednesday evening, at around sunset, reports would start piling in. Passersby motorists would report a naked female walking on the bridge of a busy highway.

The reports started light. First, she was mostly naked. Then, she was clothed on the bottom with her breasts exposed. Some RPs stated she was dancing along the side of the roadway, not impeding traffic. Others said she was praying or doing some sort of ritual chant. She was *gone on arrival* every time the officers got on the scene of the bridge.

"You know, I've seen her," Jon said.

"The nudey Judy on the bridge?" I asked.

"Yeah, I was heading home once, and I saw her dancing across the roadway, breasts bouncing in the wind," he said. "I was going to pull over and ask if I could join her."

"Then she screamed, put on her shirt, and ran away?" I laughed.

"Ha. Ha. Very funny," Jon said. "No, she—"

"I'm just going to stop you there. I know you're lying because you don't live in that direction, and I also know the joke you're trying to set me up with." I had heard him tell Megan earlier in the week. "The joke ends with you asking the woman why her boobs are so saggy. She replies that she never gets any support."

"Do you enjoy sucking all the fun and joy out of a room?" he asked me.

"Yes." I turned to my computer for another Topless Wednesday report that would inevitably be cleared as *gone on arrival*.

Finally, after about a month of this weekly ritual, the officers decided to stay in the area of the bridge. They'd be up the roadway, hidden from view of the bridge, to try to catch her. Just like clockwork, the reports started to come in. Once on scene, the officers reported seeing a middle-aged female, scantily clad with mostly exposed breasts, prancing across the bridge with a transient-looking middle-aged male behind her filming the entire thing. Confused by the situation, the officer interviewed the woman despite having any actual crime.

The woman explained that the bridge was particularly significant for her because it was the last project that her late husband worked on when he worked for the Department of Transportation. She felt particularly close to him again when she was on the bridge and wanted to look "sexy" for him. The video was for her personal archives. The officer explained to the female that although she was not committing any particular crime through her activities, she was causing quite a stir for drivers on the highway. She was empathetic and understanding, and we never heard from her again.

August 1ST, 2018 – 12 Hour Shift

A man stood alone on the side of the roadway. A bead of sweat dripped down his back as he weighed his options. Finally, after much debate, pulled the phone out of his pocket and dialed 911.

Anne, a relatively new call-taker, got the call.

After getting the caller's location, Anne asked, "What are you reporting?"

"A woman just stole my car," the RP said, panicked, voice shaken.

"Ok, how long ago did this happen?"

"Just a few minutes ago."

"Do you know who this woman is?" Anne asked.

"Uhm, kind of? We met on Facebook," he said.

"Why would she take your car?"

"I don't know, we were supposed to go on a date. I went in to grab some things from the gas station, and she took off in my car."

His story didn't seem right. Anne, although new, could tell something was off.

"Ok, where was this date supposed to happen?" she asked.

"Uhh, at the motel," he said.

I did not have much going on, so I listened in. At this point in the call, I disconnected, walked behind Anne, and started singing to the tune of Camptown Races, "Prostitute done stole your car. Doo da doo da. Prostitute done stole your car. Do de doo da day. Supposed to give you a handyyy, stole your ride instead... Prostitute done stole your car. Do de doo da day!"[4]

Anne had a challenging time keeping it together to finish the call for unknown reasons. She told me later that she about laughed on the recorded line.

I enjoy being a workplace terrorist. It brings me a level of joy that I never knew I had locked inside of me. Knowing I can throw someone off their game by making them giggle during a call makes me so happy. I have some regular targets that I know can handle it; Audrey, Carrie, and Jon, to name a few. Megan never falls for my antics and always seems slightly annoyed after, so I avoid her. Mike The Dick is undeserving of me.

"Hey, did you take that sheet on my desk?" Audrey asked. She should stop setting me up so well if she didn't love it.

"No, Audrey, I did not take a sheet on your desk," I said plainly.

"Well, there was a sheet there, and now it's gone," Audrey said.

"Ok, well, I'll ask around for you," I said and turned to the entire dispatch floor, "hey, did anyone take a sheet on Audrey's desk? Audrey said she had a sheet on her desk, and she did not take it. So which one of you took a sheet on her

---

[4] I wrote that. Prove I didn't.

desk?" I turned back and looked at Audrey, "Was it a big sheet? Normal-sized sheet?"

"A normal 8x10," she said.

She wasn't hearing it.

That just meant I had to keep going.

"Ok, everyone, it was a *normal* sheet, nothing huge, nothing crazy." I kept at it. "No one will confess to taking a sheet on Audrey's desk? Come on guys, that's pretty uncouth to take a sheet on Audrey's desk."

"Oh my god! I see what you're doing, stop!" Audrey sat down as the room broke into laughter.

She slumped down in defeat.

I am an office delight.

June 20TH, 2016 – 8 Hour Shift

North of a major intersection off the highway, in a field, late at night, we started getting reports of a topless female in the middle of the field dancing strangely.

"Why do you always get the topless calls?" Jon asked with a bit of jealousy.

"It's not like I can see them; I just get the reports," I said. "Want to see a magic trick?"

"Always."

"I don't have a single officer in service right now, but in just a few seconds, I'll magically have several. Watch." I stepped on my broadcast pedal. "City units, several reports of a female topless on the side of the roadway, dancing wildly. Not impeding traffic, callers concerned for her well-being."

"Sam 24, show me en route."

"Sam 17, show me en route."

"Charlie 20, show me en route."

"Charlie 20 isn't even a city unit. He must really care about her well-being," I said.

"They did swear an oath to protect *and* serve," Jon said.

"Oh, I have no doubt they'll do both," I chuckled.

The officers raced to the scene, and instead of finding a topless female, they found a man dressed in a full ghillie suit running across the highway.[5]

"Wait, so they didn't find the naked woman? They found a creature from the black lagoon?" Jon asked.

"Half-naked, and yeah, that's what it sounds like."

They stopped the ghillie-suited man and interviewed him. Apparently, the sightings of the topless female were accurate. However, she had returned to her house by the time the officers arrived. The ghillie-suited man was watching her. He told the officers that the woman was his wife.

"She's a witch," I read the notes on the call. "She does this during the solstice. She goes out and dances, prays and pays homage to the pagan Gods. The ghillie suit man is her husband, and he worries about her safety."

"Interesting," Jon said.

---

[5] A ghillie suit is a type of camouflage designed to resemble the background environment, such as foliage, snow, sand, etc.

"He is former military, goes out in his ghillie suit to keep an eye on her because there really are *weirdos out there*," I laughed at the irony.

The officers followed the male subject to the house and confirmed his story. In the home, there were all sorts of witch paraphernalia, and of course, the witch herself who corroborated the story with one exception. She did not know her husband was watching and that was upsetting.

"Makes sense. Weirdly, I think I'd want a woman like that," Jon said.

"Oh yeah? I thought you had a woman like that."

"What do you mean?"

"You always told me your ex-wife was a witch."

9

I love you more than coffee, but please don't make me prove it…

Dispatch: 911, where is your emergency?
Male Caller: I'm at the World Hotel.
Dispatch: Ok, and what is going on there tonight?
Male Caller: Well, my boyfriend tried to stab me with a knife.
Dispatch: Ok, is he still there?
Male Caller: Yes.
Dispatch: Does he still have the knife?
Male Caller: Yes.
Dispatch: Are you able to get away from him?
Male Caller: Yeah, I am locked in the bathroom right now.
Dispatch: Ok. *gets relevant information, name, date of birth, etc.* Has he been physically violent with you in any other way?
Male Caller: Yes, he hit me.
Dispatch: Do you need an ambulance?
Male Caller: No.
Dispatch: Does he know you've called 911?
Male Caller: No.
Dispatch: Do you think he will be violent with law enforcement.
Male Caller: I don't know. I've never seen him act this crazy before.
Loud shuffle in the background
New Voice: Who is this?
Dispatch: Hello, I'm Kyle. Who is this?
New Voice: This is James's boyfriend.
Dispatch: Ok. Have you two been arguing tonight?
New Voice: Maybe… wait, is this the police?
Dispatch: I am 911, yes. I understand you two have had a bit of a disagreement tonight.

New Voice: *starts arguing with original RP in the background*
Dispatch: Hello! Talk to me, please! Hello! HELLO?
New Voice: WHAT?
Dispatch: Can you please talk to me? Just leave him alone for now.
New Voice: What do you want?
Dispatch: What started the argument tonight?
New Voice: He was going to eat my Hot Pocket!

Crimes of passion are some of the strangest calls I get at a 911 center. Unfortunately, I have dealt with some sad and unusual domestic violence calls.

Why does it seem like we always hurt the ones we love the most? According to the National Coalition Against Domestic Violence (NCADV), on a typical day, 911 and other hotlines receive over 20,800 calls in the United States. 19% of domestic violence includes a weapon. 1 in 3 women have been physically abused by an intimate partner.

It is also noteworthy that an intimate partner has also physically abused 1 in 4 men. It is easy to start to assume based on what we are hearing.Typically, in the 911 center, a neighbor overhears the argument and calls it in.

May 17TH, 2013 – 8 Hour Shift

The neighbor could hear the yelling and screaming of a female subject and possibly two other male subjects. There was no mention of weapons, as the RP could only hear the event, she was unable to see anything.

"These types of calls stress me out." I looked over at Laura, who was reading a book.

"What have you got?"

"A domestic violence incident."

"Oh, unfortunately, you'll get used to them. We get them quite often, I'm afraid." She replaced the bookmark and swiveled in my direction. "Is there something particularly bad about this one?"

"I'm not sure. The neighbor can't see them." I recheck the system, looking for updates.

"Oh. It's not even a confirmed DV? They could be playing a game or arguing over literally anything." She picks her book back up. "It is Friday night, after all. Remember, it's not illegal to yell."

"True." I watched as the officers got on the scene. They ran the names of the people involved and advised briefly that it was, in fact, a physical domestic.

"Sam 22, we've got one in custody."

"Copy." I turned to Laura. "Well, it was a confirmed DV incident, and now they have one in custody for assault."

"Oh, that's too bad," Laura said.

I was just getting to know Laura at this point in my career, but years later, I learned that Laura grew up in a house full of domestic violence.

"Don't forget to get the paperwork for the jail started," Laura said.

Laura started working at the dispatch center a few years before I started. She is a very quiet, yet confident individual. She mostly keeps to herself and will rarely start a conversation but will always happily engage in one if started by someone else.

I found much later that her biological father was an abusive alcoholic who beat her, her mother, and her sisters. Thankfully, her mother was able to get them out of that situation and eventually married a police officer. A man whom Laura credits for inspiring her to become a dispatcher.

I started the arrest paperwork on the male subject. After the officers went en route to the jail, I learned they had the female half in custody. She was the aggressor in this case, and I assumed incorrectly.

"That's what you get when you assume! Women can be abusers too," Laura reminded me.

"As someone with many wonderful women in my life, I didn't want to believe that a woman would beat up her man. The feminist in me, though, says hell yeah, she can," I said.

"Thanks for being an ally, I guess?" Laura smiled.

Our minds are pre-programmed to make biases based on our experiences. It is a survival technique. Our primal lizard brains are designed to make snap judgments to keep us safe. This phenomenon is commonly referred to as "fight or flight."

Our ancestors running around the forest would have to make a quick decision when the bushes began to shuffle whether or not they would take off for the hills or stand their ground and fight whatever jumped out at them. We do this hundreds of times a day. However, it is generally no longer for saving our lives.

We decide quickly whether to talk to the person in the grocery store line, whom we will hire in interviews, and which route we will take home in the middle of the night.

Dispatchers go through this fight or flight several hundred times a day, except our choices and actions affect the lives of others. We are trained in this decision-making process. We are painfully aware that our actions and decisions have consequences, and we try to stay conscious of these facts to stay ahead of mistakes. Despite all of this, we remain human. We make mistakes, assumptions, and biases, which can have adverse effects.

February 19TH, 2015 – 12 Hour Shift

There are strong domestic violence laws in my state. If 911 is called regarding a DV situation and the officer finds out that it was physical in any way, they are required by law to make an arrest. It's mandatory. Sometimes, we can bend the rules, but never with domestic violence calls. Ultimately the police are bound to the laws just as everyone else.

"South units, report of a possible domestic violence situation at 2514 Melville Road. RP is a neighbor hearing banging and yelling in the unit next door. No mention of weapons," I broadcasted, then waited to see if any officers would clear their calls and go en route.

"Charlie 20, you can show me and Charlie 18 en route. Do we have any history on that address?"

"Copy en route, and that's a negative on history." This means we have never responded to this address, nor has the address called 911. We have kept legacy data on our CAD system from approximately 1998 to the present. It doesn't give us a ton of data, but it will let us know if we've been there and provide a brief synopsis of why we were there.

I read another call, checked my email, and picked up my snack pack off the floor. I grabbed a bottle of water and looked around at the other dispatchers. Apparently, it was busy everywhere but my radio. Another report crossed my desk. Uninteresting, it was another vehicle prowl. It can hold until I have an officer available.

I checked on the possible domestic violence call. Both units have been on the scene for about 10 minutes, and I haven't heard from them.

"Charlie 20 or Charlie 18, status?" I broadcasted.

"Charlie 18, we have one in custody. Can you have the sergeant call me on my work cell?"

"Copy one in custody, and Charlie 2, did you copy the request?" [1]

"Affirmative. Calling now," Charlie 2 said.

Odd.

This could be entertaining. I looked again at the call to see if they had run any names. Nothing. At this point, all I could do was wait and see. Finally, after a few minutes, Charlie 20 came up on the air.

---

[1] If I was unclear, Charlie 2 is the sergeant.

"Charlie 20 to dispatch, Charlie 18 is going to remain on scene, and you can show me en route to the jail."

"Copy," I was worried that a parent might be hurting a child. Usually, they would ask me to make a CPS callout by now. So it seems unlikely.

"Charlie, 20 to dispatch. Can you also get me the number for the on-call prosecutor and have that ready for me when I get to the jail?"

Uh, "Affirmative."

I pulled up my emails and filtered through my saved files. We get an updated monthly spreadsheet of who is on-call at an extensive list of agencies. Emergencies happen 24 hours a day, but they're not so common that we need someone staffed 24 hours a day. Certain agencies have on-call availability. Judges – both superior and lower courts like traffic, medical examiner's office, child protective services (CPS), and of course, the prosecutor's office, to name a few.

Some agencies pass around a cell phone instead of making us have a list. I prefer that option over hunting down their ever-changing phone numbers. I located the needed phone number and waited for the officer to reach the jail.

Charlie 20 dropped off his suspect in the jail to be processed and booked by the jail staff and then came into the dispatch center to get the number from me.

"Hey dude, got that number for you. What's going on?" I asked.

"Oh, god, it's actually horrible." If Charlie 20 says it's horrible, it must be bad. "We get on scene and hear the yelling from the driveway. We knock, and a 76 old man answers the door. I explain why we are there. He explains that he has a 57-year-old son who is developmentally delayed, and he's being particularly difficult for him that night. He is his son's only caretaker, and he was refusing to get ready for bed."

"Wow, that is not where I thought that was going," I said.

"No, us either. The old guy explains that they got into a little scuffle, and he admits that he hit his son. Now that he's told us that, our hands our tied. We are required to make the arrest. I'm not risking my job or life over it."

Charlie 20 was correct. They could be arrested and charged with failure to protect. Officers take domestic violence very seriously, as they should.

"I screened the arrest with the sergeant and asked if we could cite and release on scene. He said no, we're not allowed to do that. They have to be brought in and booked."

"Yikes, and no one else can care for his son tonight?" I asked.

"Negative. That's why Charlie 18 is still there. I will try to talk to the prosecutor, explain the situation, and see if we can take him back home tonight. Otherwise, we have to figure out an emergency custody situation for his son."

"Wow, well, good luck." I handed him the piece of paper with the phone number. The prosecutor was sympathetic; however, there was a minimum amount of time they had to remain in jail for a *cooling-off period* before someone could be released. The prosecutor agreed that they would not pursue charges. I assisted again by finding an after-hours number for adult protective services, and we got the son an emergency placement in a group home for the evening.

Not an ideal situation. Considering how much worse it could have been without a compassionate officer, I'm glad Charlie 20 handled it with such grace.

August 7ᵀᴴ, 2018 – 12 Hour Shift

Ma'am, I understand you're upset, but when you scream, I can't understand you." I've been struggling for about ten minutes with this distraught elderly female. "That's much better. Thank you. Uh-huh. Ok. Is this happening right now?"

"Yes!"

"Ok, where is this happening? At what address?" I asked, already very tired of this phone call at this point.

"I don't know."

"Ok, let me recap this entire situation to ensure I understand correctly. You're seeing a woman mercilessly beating her daughter. You're seeing this all right now but don't know where it's happening? Do I have that correct?"

Apparently, I have it all.

"Ok, so how are you seeing this? Uh-huh... ok...

well, that does not mean that it's happening right now. No, unfortunately, there isn't anything that we can do. No. We have no idea where they are. It's a recording. Yeah. So, it could have happened years ago. I know. Uh-huh. I know. Yep. Again, I'm sorry, but no, there is nothing we will be able to do about that. Uh-huh, goodbye."

The entire room was staring at me.

"Old lady watching a video on YouTube," I said.

Everyone immediately understood the conversation and turned back to their computers.

I got unplugged and went to the kitchen for a snack on my first coffee break. A group of dispatchers hung out in the hallway, laughing and chatting. Laura was among them. Apparently, we were both doing overtime today. I walked up to the group after grabbing my apple.

"What are we laughing about?" I asked.

"We're taking a poll that might be based on a real-life event," Allen said.

"What's the poll?" I asked. "Also, whose real-life event, that may alter my decision."

"How would you feel if your significant other replaced your shower curtain with an Art Deco curtain with a drawing of Jeff Goldblum holding a monkey?" Allen looked at Maria, who turned bright red.

"I would be upset. My bathroom, particularly my shower, is my happy place, and I wouldn't want Jeff Goldblum and a monkey staring at me in my happy place," Laura said.

"I would probably laugh at the whole thing, but I'd probably take it down," Jessica said.

"You can't take that down! I would be honored to have such a masterpiece in my house," Allen was the cute eccentric. Always leaving us, never knowing when he's kidding or not.

The crowd turned to me.

"Oh, uh, I don't know. I guess I would just be happy to be in a relationship." Like a fart in an elevator, I dropped it and walked away.

May 21ST, 2015 – 12 Hour Shift

It started as a routine call. A woman was being harassed by a male subject in the parking lot of a motel. It was down south, almost at the county line. The RP did not know the subject and stated only the female was a motel guest, but she appeared to know the male subject. We typically send one officer for this type of response; no weapons were involved, and they were not physical with each other.

A few minutes later, we received another call from a male neighbor of the harassed woman at the motel. His demeanor was calm, precise, and matter-of-fact. He provided us a little more detail about the situation. The neighbor advised the woman was staying at the motel because the RP got the room for her. Apparently, her husband routinely beat her. The neighbor was trying to help this woman financially and physically by getting her out of the house. With this new information, I sent a backing unit down, with the first one already en route.

"Oh, this is getting spicy," I said.

"What have you got?" MaryAnne, our newest dispatcher, slid near to read over my shoulder. "Are you familiar with these people?"

"Nope. I haven't heard of any of them before. I only had one unit going, but considering they allegedly have a history of physical abuse, I added a second unit." I pointed to the screen. "Unfortunately, they are both quite far away."

"Oh yeah, that's really far south," MaryAnne said.

MaryAnne and I got along great. She asked for tips, tricks, and for me to tell her if I got anything more significant. She learned by watching and doing. The same as myself.

It was a thirty-minute drive to the motel for the inbound units. At least ten minutes had passed since the neighbor had called the first time.

The RP called back.

This time, he was still calm and precise, but the call-taker could tell the RP was annoyed at how long it took for the deputies to get on the scene. He ended the call by saying, "You better get there before I do."

"Wow. Did you see the update?" MaryAnne asked.

"Yeah. People make all sorts of threats to 911. I don't know if it is an attempt to make their call seem more important? Maybe to make sure the units will respond faster? It doesn't work that way. Responding units can only go as fast as they can go. They need to be safe, too," I explained. "Making threats to either law enforcement or others can result in additional charges being filed. Especially since 911 lines are recorded. This probably won't result in a charge because there wasn't a specific threat of violence."

I didn't know how wrong I was about to be.

Another ten minutes passed, and we received another call from the motel. Again, it was the male neighbor.

"He is dead. I don't like wife-beaters or baby rapists," his calm demeanor never faulted.

"Excuse me?" the call-taker asked in disbelief.

"I shot him right between the eyes. I warned you to beat me here," he said without missing a beat.

"Where is the gun?" asked the call-taker.

"It is with the bartender. When you get here, I will be at the bar having a drink," he said before disconnecting.

I updated responding units, then started additional units making sure the Sergeant went as well.

I was also kind of in disbelief.

"Do you want me to start an ambulance response for you?" MaryAnn interrupted my internal processing.

"Yes, that's a great idea. Make sure to tell them to stage. The suspect is still technically on scene and still armed," I said.

She was going to do great things. Usually, I have to prompt the other dispatchers to assist me with these details.

"Jackson, do you have a murder over there?" Audrey stood up from the supervisor's desk.

"Yeaaaa," I said sheepishly. "You might want to start making your notifications."

"Why are you such a shit magnet?" Audrey said.

The police arrested the neighbor and charged him with murder. I found out later from the responding officers that the guy finished his drink, willingly volunteered himself, and confessed to everything. He was released on bail later that evening.

I kept up on this highly publicized case. A little more than a year later, after due process, a jury found him not guilty on all charges.

December 25TH, 2016 – 12 Hour Shift

Holidays are prime days for domestic violence. It's one of the reasons I don't like Christmas. People see family that they avoid for the rest of the year. As a result, the old drama gets brought back to the surface, temperatures run high, and alcohol is often involved.

"You don't like Christmas, Jackson?" Mike The Dick asked, overhearing our conversation.

"I don't. I get around it by not celebrating, and I never mind working the holiday," I said.

"So, I can't say Merry Christmas to you?"

He's always looking for a fight.

"You can absolutely say Merry Christmas to me if you want to," I said, trying my best to be civil.

"Well, I don't want to upset you by saying Merry Christmas."

"Why would it upset me, Mike?"

"If you don't like Christmas and you don't celebrate it, you'd get mad at me if I told you Merry Christmas."

I think you can guess how Mike votes.

"Ok, well, before two minutes ago, you wouldn't have known I don't celebrate Christmas. So therefore, if you said Merry Christmas to me, I would not be offended." I paused.

Mike The Dick started to speak, but I cut him off.

"However, now that you know I'm not a Christian and I don't celebrate Christmas, saying Merry Christmas would, in fact, upset me. Because I would *know* that you were trying to make me upset."

I could almost see the poor wheel in his head trying to turn.

"So you're not a Christian either?"

"Correct."

Please say something stupid, Mike. I have a lot of witnesses watching this.

"Well, ok. Hope you have a nice... Sunday then." He walked away defeated.

"Thank you. Happy Sunday to you, too, Mike." Then under my breath so, my closest coworkers could hear, "You dick."

"Don't worry, he's getting coal in his stockings," Carrie said.

I wasn't even sure she was listening. I just laughed. I didn't know what else to say after that.

My Christmas gift would come a little bit later.

We got a 911 call from a woman who stated her husband had choked her, kicked her, went outside, busted up her vehicle, and then took off. Police arrived on the scene within minutes. She had an obvious neck injury and a scrape down the front of her chest. She was in rough shape. Her children were home, and the eldest son attempted to assist his mother by jumping on the father's back and pulling his hair to get him off his mother. The RP didn't know where her husband would have gone, but she gave his vehicle description and license plate.

Twenty minutes passed before officers located the subject's vehicle at the grocery store. The officers cleared the grocery store after calling for backup and securing the front doors. The suspect was not inside, and the vehicle was cold to the touch. It had been there for a while.

"It sucks that they didn't find him," Mike The Dick said.

"It's not over just yet," I said. "I did some more digging on previous 911 calls from this guy. He owns the Crab Restaurant on 25th Street. I'm working with Officer Benton to set up a sting operation."

"Don't waste your time. It's not going to work," Mike is not only a dick, he doesn't think I'm good at my job. Either that, or he knows I'm good at my job but dislikes me because I don't do things the way *he* does.

"The problem with long-time abusers is that they think they can get away with anything. Unfortunately, this was not the first time this man beat up his wife," I said.

It rarely is.

In fact, most incidences of domestic violence go unreported to law enforcement. By the time it *is* reported to law enforcement by a victim, it is usually because the victim is at their breaking point.

"I'm going for my own little Christmas miracle here," I said.

"It doesn't work if you don't celebrate Christmas," Mike The Dick said.

I'm not touching that with a 10-foot pole.

I went back to work on my sting.

This husband abused his wife for years. She reported that it started as verbal threats and intimidations and eventually escalated to a slap across the face. They had kids together, she did not work, she had no way to get out, and he exploited this fact.

The suspect had no idea that the police were looking for him. Throughout the years, his violence would steadily increase to the point of nearly killing her. Since she never dared to call 911, why would he think this time would be any different?

We exploited this to our benefit.

The officers set their patrol cars up the street from the suspect's business. Four officers walked around the backside and hid at the rear entrance to the restaurant. I placed one officer in front of the business, and then I made a call to the business's alarm monitoring center. We had them call the suspect to inform him that there was an unsecured door at the business, and we needed him to respond to secure it. At this point, the suspect would know that there would be a police officer on the scene to meet him about a possible burglary at the business.

It worked like a charm.

Within fifteen minutes, our subject walked right into his cuffs. He was upset and felt deceived. His on-scene defense was that the fight was mutual, and she beat him up as often and as severely as he beat her. The only difference is his lack of wounds. He seemed to be in perfect condition aside from being under the influence of alcohol. The officers charged him with felony assault and took him to jail.

"Ha! It worked. We got him," I applauded myself loud enough for Mike The Dick to hear.

"Well, I don't know if what you did was even legal," Mike said.

Why can't he just take the win? When one of us wins, the whole team wins. A man who just beat his wife nearly to death was taken off the streets.

"Three officers and a sergeant seemed to think it was a perfectly good and *legal* plan," I snapped back. "This was truly a team effort. Speaking of, thank you, Laura, for calling the alarm company for me. We got him."

"Oh, yay! I'm glad that worked." Laura high-fived me. "I'm glad to assist wherever I can."

"That's because you're a team player, and I appreciate you."

I could not lay it on any thicker for Mike The Dick. He had nothing more to say. I count his silence as my second Christmas miracle.

Unfortunately, a month later, one of my officers reported that he pulled over a vehicle for speeding, and there they were. The same husband and wife got back together.

"God. I don't understand why she took him back." I felt defeated.

"Many reasons contribute to this. The victim loves the abuser. They got married for a reason, and at one point, she must have loved him, and maybe on some level still does and always will. Sometimes, a contributing factor is a lack of self-confidence. Sometimes the victim feels like they can't do any better," Laura said. "Occasionally, they just accept the abuse as an unavoidable part of being in a relationship. Perhaps they grew up in a house filled with domestic violence, and that is all they have ever known."

"I have never thought of it like that," I said, reflecting on my own household upbringing. "My parents definitely fought. I think that's just a normal part of being in any relationship. However, I never saw physical violence. I guess I should count myself lucky."

"You really should. I grew up in a very violent household," Laura said, testing the waters.

"Oh really? I'm sorry. That must have been tough. I bet it continues to be tough working in this line of work," I said.

"It can be. I've had a lot of therapy and have worked on a lot with my parents and my own feelings of guilt," Laura said.

"Oh?" I paused. "Well, that makes you a powerful ally for these victims. You can empathize deeply and contribute to the conversation in a way some of us can't. I am glad I get to learn from your example."

"Aww. Thanks," Laura said. "It is a complex system, and there is no one-size-fits-all reasoning behind it."

"I bet."

"Other contributing factors to domestic violence include isolationism, fear of homelessness or having no place to go, economic dependence, threats from the abuser, and danger of leaving in general. Abusers take full advantage of their control over their victims. Often, the abusers have full control over the finances. They exploit these factors to ensure that their victim cannot leave. Society's lack of understanding about the dynamics of domestic violence is one of the greatest obstacles a victim faces," Laura said.

"I remember learning about financial abuse in the academy," I said. "I'd never considered most situations before learning about them."

"It is the bulk of why my mother stayed for as long as she did. She was a stay-at-home mom for so long. She didn't have access to any resources or money to break away. It wasn't until she started her part-time job at the church that she met a support group. They assisted her with housing and getting us out of that situation." Tears start to well up in her eyes.

"She sounds like an absolute powerhouse of a woman. I am glad that she was such a champion for you." I put my hand on Laura's shoulder.

"She's my hero."

May 9TH, 2017 – 12 Hour Shift

Not all domestic violence calls are about intimate partners. To be considered a domestic situation, the subjects must only be related by proxy; siblings, parent, child, or even roommate situations. Not all domestic violence occurs in the home; sometimes, it extends into the workplace.

On Tuesday afternoon at around 13:00 hours, I got a call from a business line. I heard a slight shuffle, and then the line disconnected. As you know by now, this is an everyday event. I called the number back, and it was a pet shop.

"The Pet Shop, Brenda speaking, how may I help you?"

"Hi, Brenda, this is 911; we just received a call from this number. Do you have an emergency?" I asked.

"Uhm," A long uncomfortable pause. "That was probably my manager calling."

"Ok, is your manager having an emergency?" With her awkward pause, I got the feeling something was going on.

"Uhm, I don't know." The line cut off; I heard a brief shuffling of phones.

"Hello?" a new voice answered.

"Hi there, this is 911. We just received a call from this number. Do you have an emergency?" I asked.

"No," stated a female abruptly.

"Ok, you're sure you do not need police, fire, or medical?" I asked.

"Nope. Everything is fine here." She was gruff.

"Alright, can I get your name? I need to log it in my call," I said.

"Connie, I'm the manager."

"Ok, Connie, have a safe day."

I decided to send the police because anyway. The call didn't feel right—call it, dispatcher's intuition.

I was correct.

Connie's husband was on the scene, they were fighting in the manager's office loudly. The employees attempted to call 911 on her, and Becky intervened.

Connie had been verbally abusive to her husband and employees for some time. She was arrested, providing the employees some temporary relief. I don't know what happened to Connie after that. I hope she sought out some counseling and learned from it.

If you need a lot of closure in your life, this is not the job for you. One method dispatchers use to combat this issue is assuming that everything ended well and everyone had a great day. If we sat there and stewed over outcomes, we would be driven to a madhouse after only a week on this job. We are fortunate enough to get some closure on major events, but not always.

November 25TH, 2019 – 12 Hour Shift

Late one evening, a mother called to report that she had not heard from her son in over a week. The RP advised that her son has a history of drug abuse, and it is not uncommon for him to take off for days at a time. The RP advised that he usually rides off on his bicycle, as he does not have a valid driver's license. He then binges on his drug of choice in the woods. She was more concerned this time because the bicycle was at his ex-girlfriend's house, and she had not seen him in three days. I looked to see Devon was the call taker.

"Hey, I just wanted to talk about this missing person call quickly." I realized this sounded like I was scolding him, so I added, "You did an excellent job at getting all the pertinent information, it's just a lot of information, so I thought it would be easier if we chatted instead of messaged."

"Oh, for sure." His shoulders sink. He was ready to be yelled at.

I felt bad.

"Do we know why it was so concerning that the bicycle was left at his ex's house?" I asked.

"Apparently, it's his only mode of transportation. She lives kind of far away from any neighbor, and, weirdly, his bike is there, but her son is not."

"Ah, that makes sense." I looked over the call again, searching for something else to compliment him on to ease my guilt. "Ok, good job getting the clothing description of what he was last seen wearing."

"Thanks."

I started the missing person report. About ten minutes later, the mother called back to update us that she received a phone call from a friend who stated he had seen her son at the grocery store the day before. After that, the mother felt at ease and canceled the missing person report.

"Now she wants to cancel the report," Devon said from behind me.

"Yeah, I saw that." I shrugged. "Weird. She'll know her son the best, I guess. It also makes less work for us. So we'll call it a win."

"I just don't feel right about it," he continued.

"Oh? Which part?" asked.

"I don't know. Something feels off," Devon shrugged. "I just have a gut feeling that we're going to find his body in the woods."

"Yikes. Well, I'll keep an eye out for dead body in the woods calls, and we'll see if you're right."

I should not make these jokes.

I never learn.

About an hour later, we got a call from a hysterical woman. We could barely understand what she was saying. Thankfully, the call-taker, Brandon, knew her *in real life* and could get out the necessary information.

This was the ex-girlfriend of the former missing, not missing, adult son. She was calling to inform us that she had found him.

Dead.

"Well, your Spidey-senses were spot on tonight, Devon." I walked up behind him while leaving for break. "We found him."

"Dead?"

"Yep."

"In the woods?"

"Actually, no," I said. "He was found by his ex-girlfriend. She was quite escalated, but Brandon knows her in real-life and thankfully got the call. After she calmed down, Brandon could ascertain that she and the missing subject, Charlie, had been having relationship problems for the past couple of months. They broke up about a month ago, and she started seeing someone new."

"Yikes," Devon said.

"Oh, it gets worse." I continued, "Three days ago, Charlie called the ex-girlfriend. He told her he was in a bad way and requested to stay at her house for a few days. She reluctantly agreed. She would not be home anyway. She was staying at the new boyfriend's house that night."

"Oh god, did he hang himself in her house or something?"

"Oh no. She's been home for two days at this point. She would have seen a hanging guy two days ago. Anyway, he was not there when she got home. She didn't think much of it. She assumed he only needed a place to sleep. She also knows about his drug abuse and figured he'd gone off and on a bender."

"Ok, so then where did she find him?" Devon asked.

"Well, she calls her new boyfriend over. They searched the wooded area up the road where he'd gone on previous benders. Nothing." I swipe my arms, calling an 'out' for dramatic effect. "She and the new boyfriend spend the next two nights together at her place. Tonight, they started to notice a smell. It's not that big of a trailer, and there aren't a lot of places to look. Apparently, her bed is one of those Murphy-style beds with storage below."

"NO!" Devon covered his mouth.

"She and her new boyfriend had slept on top of Charlie's dead body for two nights."

Devon was speechless.

"Talk about the ultimate revenge. She will never sleep in a bed again without thinking about Charlie."

10

Fake It Until You Make It & The Art Of Confidence And Incompetence

radio transmission

Dispatch: Dispatch to city units, a report of a disturbance at the Roadway Pub.

Officer: Go ahead.

Dispatch: RP is an employee and states they kicked out a subject for being disruptive when they refused to serve him because he was already overly intoxicated, now causing a scene outside.

Officer: En route.

Dispatch: RP is now stating the subject has been locked out of the business and is attempting to break the door down.

Officer: Do we have a description?

Dispatch: White male, 30's 6 foot 1, 190, wearing a white shirt and jeans.

Officer: Ok, do we have anything further?

Dispatch: *confused* RP advised he is still at the door… now he is ripping off the side of the doorframe.

Officer: Ok, do we have any further description?

Dispatch: ….it will be the drunk male ripping down the door….

Officer: uhm…. Copy that.

I love my officers, but sometimes they can be like our children. A significant part of dispatch is thinking ahead of the officers. Something that is difficult to teach to new people. We have a flow, an order, and a system in place for every single scenario. We make it so that understanding each other is easy.

Transmission A responds with transmission B, and transmission C replies with transmission D. We read back people, vehicles, wanted subjects, etc., in the same patterns.

For instance, in vehicle returns, we use CYMBALS. This stands for Color, Year, Make, Body, Additional descriptive items, License and State. The suspect vehicle will be a Grey, 1999 Toyota 4D, with front-end damage, license ABC123, out of Missouri. We get used to hearing the transmissions the same way every time. Sometimes, our officers forget the system and complicate our jobs for no reason.

When an officer goes out on a traffic stop, we get a location and a license plate. It comes in this order, so we can quickly type it into our CAD system. Then, we run the license plate to see what vehicle they just stopped.[1] Traffic stops have the highest rate of volatile incidents; this includes officer-involved shootings. Therefore, it is imperative that we always know the officer's location and the vehicle they stopped. Some officers mumble, some officers have strange cadences or accents, and some just do not know where they are.

May 15TH, 2017 – 12 Hour Shift

The on-duty sergeant of the sheriff's office went out on a traffic stop. He told me that he was at milepost seven on

---

[1] It returns the vehicle registration, any stolen hits, or any violent offender info related to that vehicle.

Center Road and gave me the license plate of the vehicle he stopped. After running the plate through the system, I also got the return on the registered owner, and it showed he had an active warrant.

"Dispatch to Charlie 2 with warrant info."

"Driver has a gun! Gun!"

"Charlie 2 out with a subject armed with a gun, I need more units en route, and we'll hold the air.[2] Charlie 2 is at Center Road mile marker 7." My heart was in my throat, my fingers trembling, and I could not hear a soul around me.

If anyone said anything to me, I have no idea. I just watched my screen as six officers went en route to back the sergeant at milepost seven on Center Road.

One was only a mile away. It felt like an eternity before he arrived on the scene.

"I'm at mile marker 7 and not seeing Charlie 2."

Panic set in, and I replayed the transmission to ensure I heard his location correctly.

"Charlie 2, can you verify your location?"

No response.

"Charlie 2. Status and location." The only noise on the radio was the beeping from the priority-marker tones.

"Charlie 2's GPS locator is not working. I verified on the playback that he should be at Center Road mile marker 7," I said.

---

[2] When the air is held, no one can speak except for me and the unit needing the air held. There are audible tones that beep every eight seconds to remind everyone.

Per policy, their GPS locators must always be on and functioning. I live in a rural area, and it doesn't always get a signal. I could not ping his vehicle directly.

"Charlie 17 to dispatch. I've been out to mile marker 9 and have not seen him. So I'm turning back around and double-check my way to marker 6."

"Sam 20, I'm going to check the parallel highway and look at mile marker 7 there."

I had not thought to go to the main highway since it was a couple miles east of Center Road.

"Sam 20, I've got him here. We have one proned-out."

Success!

The sergeant had given the incorrect location at the time of his stop.

"Copy. Status of Charlie 2?"

Please let him be ok.

"He's good. Incoming units approach from the north. Line of fire will be to the south."

"Copy incoming units from the north. Line of fire pointing south."

After a few more minutes, I got the best broadcast I could have hoped for.

"Charlie 2 to dispatch, one in custody with no incident. You can open the air." The sergeant was ok, and no one was injured.

It was entirely the sergeant's fault. He gave his location incorrectly when he stopped the vehicle. Yet, I could not help but feel guilty. Everything ended up being ok with the sergeant; he was able to coerce the individual into putting his gun down and take him into custody without a struggle. He worked with the suspect, trying to develop a rapport and not get himself killed, so he could not answer my radio traffic. This is why we always stress the importance of location. We cannot send help if we do not know where you are.

This goes for the first responders as well as you callers out there.

June 25TH, 2019 – 8 Hour Shift

Oh my god, and this is why I call him Mike The Meathead," Carrie said, laughing hysterically at her screen.

"Oh man, what happened now?" I asked.

Mike the Meathead was one of my favorite officers on the city force. He is your stereotypical jock-type but not a handsome guy. Sweetest man in the world, a very empathetic cop, a loving family man, very swarthy; the kind of man who wears a toolbelt but couldn't spell *toolbelt*.

You know the type.

"We got a report of a man on the floor in his house. His friend was there to pick him up for a doctor's appointment, and he was not answering the door, so he went around and peered into a window and saw his friend on the floor. He called 911, and we got the ambulances started," Carrie said. "After the EMTs arrived, they requested law enforcement to get into the house. The closest officer was Mike."

Carrie starts to laugh.

"Mike gets on the scene of the house. He marched right up to the door and kicked it in, splitting it in half," Carrie's nearly in tears.

"Oh god. Let me guess, the wife or something was home?" I asked.

"Oh no. No one was home," Carrie snorted. "He gets on the radio and asks me where the EMTs are. I asked Jon where they were." Jon was working the fire radio that morning. "He tells me they're waiting for him at the front of the house. So, I passed the info on."

I'm confused.

Why would he kick in the door and then ask where the EMTs are? The friend should also be there, right?

"Why didn't he see the EMTs?" I asked.

"He kicked in the door of the wrong house!" My jaw dropped.

"Oh my god!" I covered my mouth with both of my hands. "Were the people of the wrong house at home?"

"I don't think so," Carrie said. "Apparently, he went to 417 C Street when the address was 417 D Street. He was quite upset and tried to blame me for the fact that he had gone to the incorrect house. I corrected him. I said, not only did I clarify and say D- David Street, you should have noticed when you got on the scene that there was no ambulance out front.'"

"Woah. He must be completely beside himself if he's trying to put that on you. Mike is a sweetheart." I couldn't believe it.

"Yeah, he apologized immediately for trying to throw me under the bus." Carrie isn't one to hold a grudge anyway. She's been at this for too long to take anything personally.

Mike was upset with himself for making a hilariously embarrassing error and was looking to deflect it on Carrie. He did not live that one down for quite a while.

"Wait, what happened with the dude on the floor?"

"Oh, Mike got to kick in another door. The right door this time," Carrie said.

"Well, that's good," I said. "And the man on the floor?"

"Heh?" Jon asked.

"The guy on the floor? Was he ok?"

"Oh. Gosh no. DRT," Jon said.

We in the business know DRT to mean Dead Right There. Meaning absolutely no chance of resuscitation.

"I'm just curious what Mike will do for the people who now have no front door?"

"Mike's sergeant is en route, and they're going to leave a note and have the fire department board up the hole," Carrie said. "Oh, speaking of, can you send a unit for that, Jon?"

"On it." Jon turned back around.

"Will the city have to pay for the damages?" I asked Carrie.

"Most definitely," she said. "I know they have insurance for certain damages caused by the police or any other city worker. For instance, a utility worker accidentally dropped a tree on someone's house. That went through the city's insurance. I'm assuming a similar policy will take care of it."

"If not, they can sue," I said.

"Oh, they probably will." I never followed up to find out if they actually did sue the city or not. I'm not even sure how to find that out. Accidents happen, even to us.

October 28TH, 2018 – 12 Hour Shift

Police officers are always pretending to be firefighters. This annoys both dispatchers and actual firefighters.

We received a report of a possible carbon monoxide leak inside a home. This is a common event—most people forget they even have a carbon monoxide detector. They will beep when they have an alarm, malfunction, or are low on batteries. When we get these reports, we can ask the caller if they are feeling ill, faint, or dizzy, and we can ask the caller if they would like to evacuate for their safety. Due to potential liability, we cannot tell the caller what to do.

The RP decided that the beep was more intermittent, she was not feeling ill, and it was most likely due to a battery or wire issue. She made the choice to remain in her home. We toned out the fire department and got them started to assist. The city's police department requests informational dispatches on any aid or fire calls so they are aware of them.

"Dispatch to City Units, information only, fire has been advised of a CO_2 alarm at 123 Main Street, information at 19:54 hours."

"Have the occupants evacuated?" asked Officer Finkowski, the firefighter wannabe.

"Negative, stated it was likely due to a battery malfunction. We're toning the fire department to assist with replacing a battery," I said.

"Well, they can't be sure it is just a battery issue," Finkowski said indignantly.

At this point, I thought, *you can't be sure that it is not a battery issue*, but instead, I responded more appropriately with "received."

"You need to call them back and tell them they need to get out NOW," Finkowski said.

There are several problems with this approach. First of which, the officer forgot his role. Dispatch tells him where to go and what to do, not the other way around. Secondly, the actually trained professionals in carbon monoxide detection were also en route to the scene and were not concerned about her not evacuating.

"Received," I said. It was my turn to be indignant.

I called back to the poor woman and explained what the officer had told me. She chuckled and stated she was just fine and would remain in her home. I wished her a safe day and waited smugly for the officer to get on the scene.

"Did you hear all that?" I said.

Phoebe was working the fire radio that night. "What?" she asked, putting her book down.

Phoebe is more of a day-shifter, and I don't know her very well. But I assumed she'd like this story. So I explained the back-and-forth I just had with Officer Finkowski.

"Wow. The nerve of some of these guys. Is he just jealous he can't drive the engine?"

"That's my theory," I chuckled.

"I'm going to let my guys know that a prospective firefighter, Officer Finkowski, is en route to assist them." She turned around to broadcast on her air to Engine 15.

Thankfully, the fire department beat him there. Officer Finkowski burst through the door and was ready to assist in any way that he could. The firefighter looked at the officer, fully aware of the events that had transpired with dispatch. They thanked him for his service and said with a smile, "I know I am just a simple firefighter, but I think I can handle this battery replacement by myself."

Humility is an essential lesson for all of us.[3]

February 20TH, 2016 – 12 Hour Shift

There is a technology flaw with our CAD system. The moment a CFS is created, anyone on the system can see it. The officers sometimes get bored and jump on the call. They start en route to the address the second it's entered into the system. This can be bothersome for several reasons.

Firstly, the address given may not be where the event is happening. This is because we do not have enough information yet.

Secondly, the caller might be reporting something which occurred several days ago. The caller might not even be at the

---

[3] Don't worry, I have a ton of embarrassing stories about the hose draggers in the next chapter.

address on the call anymore. They could have moved to a secondary location.

Lastly, the dispatcher does not generally read the call until a Type Code is entered for the call.[4] Therefore, if the officer asks questions about the call before it's complete, they will catch everyone off guard.

To every rule, there is an exception. We sometimes put in calls with no information just to get units started. They are priority one calls that have the potential for death. We can immediately tell that something is wrong and must begin units quickly.

For example, if we get a report of domestic violence with a gun, we have the Type Code DVW, Domestic Violence Weapon. We immediately know there is a volatile situation, and we need to start units. We will update units with information while they are driving.

If we get a report of domestic violence with a gun, but it happened last week, we do not put "DVW" in the call type field. Instead, we leave it blank until we have all the pertinent information and send out the more appropriate "DVR" – Domestic Violence Report – the word "report" signaling that it is *not* in progress.

Officers are constantly reminded not to jump calls, yet they can't help themselves.

"Arg," I yelled and slammed my mouse angrily.

---

[4] A Type Code is a short-hand summation of the call. For example, DISTV would be a Disturbance with the V at the end notating, domestic violence. A DIST is a disturbance with no DV aspects. ROB for robbery and THFT for a theft. You get the idea.

I'm pretty sure all dispatchers do this. Correct me if I'm wrong.

"Uh oh, what happened?" Laura looked up.

"It's actually a little comical, albeit annoying," I said. "One of our regulars, Mr. Grey called and reported a rape of a female at an address in the city, 143 A Street. He was vivid with the details and stated that it was in progress." [5]

I had a lot of experience with this caller, as did Laura.

The call taker jotted down the RP's report into the CFS. However, he did not assign it a Type Code just yet.

"I hadn't even read the call yet," Laura said. "Mr. Grey? Enough said on that front." She laughed and turned back to her screen.

"Mary 17 took it upon himself to go en route, lights on and sirens blaring," I said and shook my head. "He started asking me about more details in the call. I had no idea what he was talking about. Mary 22 perked up, and he also started going en route."

I played back the recording for Laura.

Mary 17 queued his radio, "Is there a weapon involved in that assault in progress?"

"Confirm which assault in progress?" I asked, puzzled by the question. I scanned my screen for an in-progress call.

"The sexual assault at 123 A Street," Mary 17 shouted.

"We have no CFS at that address," I sounded annoyed and confused.

---

[5] Remember our routine callers who report things that happen only in their head.

I ended the recording and looked at Laura. "At this point, I heard his agitated voice. I explained to the Mary cars that he had jumped the call. We were on the phone with one of our regulars, and he needs to stand down."

Laura's laughter was interrupted by another broadcast in my ear.

"Mary 1, show me en route to the Sexual Assault in progress on A street as well." Mary 1 is a sergeant.

"Lord, this is blowing up," I said, and another unit piped up before I could broadcast anything else.

"Mary 12, you can show me en route as well."

With my deepest father-like voice, I said, "Dispatch to ALL UNITS, there is NO assault in progress. This is a report from Mr. Grey, a known daily caller who has not yet been assigned a Type Code. All units stand down."

Mary 1 was not pleased with his units. I heard they got an earful later at the precinct.

I never got an apology.

I don't hold grudges. I just embarrass them in a novel.

July 2ND, 2019 – 12 Hour Shift

As I have hammered home, location is the most important thing to a 911 dispatcher. If we do not know where you are, we can't send help.

Second to location is who. Who, is sometimes convoluted. I need to know whom the officer is contacting. I can ascertain this information from a license plate by running the registered

197

owner. Sure, someone else could be driving the vehicle, but 80% of the time, the driver is the vehicle's registered owner. The number of people is also essential. I never want my officer outnumbered by more than two.

"I'm out with two," I might send another unit to start in that direction.

"I'm out with three," and I am sending another officer.

"I'm out with four," or more, and I am sending that additional officer with a priority response, including lights and sirens.

It was almost the 4th of July, and I had an officer roll up to a Minor in Possession or MIP party, and the first thing I hear is, "I'm out with fifty."

"Confirm out with fifteen?" I must have misheard it.

"Negative, that's five-zero," he stated clearly.

The officer arrived on the scene at a house crawling with drunken teenagers. This would later be described as a clip from *The Walking Dead*. I immediately sent everyone I had available to go and assist the officer.

The first officer on the scene started corralling them like sheep and decided it would be fun to run each one of them through me. Running each of those kids through the system took me over an hour. I wondered why.

Most were not even old enough to have instructor's permits, let alone active warrants for their arrests. Then, to make it worse, he had me start calling the parents of these juveniles to have them picked up.

The first officer arrived on the scene at 03:27 in the morning; I did not finish making my phone calls until 06:43. I never slept so hard in all my years as I did after that shift.

August 27ND , 2017 – 12 Hour Shift

What are you doing there, Laura?" Carrie asked over her shoulder.

"I'm studying for the Mensa Exam," she showed Carrie the cover of her book.

"Oh? What's that?" Carrie asked.

"Something you clearly wouldn't qualify for," Jon interrupted.

"Hardee har har," Carrie said.

"She gets to be an official card-carrying genius if she passes," I explained. "I don't know that I'd want to be a card-carrying genius working this job. I mean, how depressing would that be? I like being a moron. It makes my life decisions make more sense."

"Wow. I didn't think of it like that," Jon looked stunned. "You really are smart."

"NO, I'M NOT," I walked to my terminal.

I sat down at my computer. I was working south radio that night. It's my favorite radio because although it can be messy, it's usually busy and makes the time go by much faster. The call came in at 19:34 in the evening, it was summer, so it was still light out. The call read that someone was acting loud and belligerent in the neighborhood. The RP stated that the

199

subject was under the influence of alcohol and possibly narcotics.

The first RP stated the male subject was screaming and yelling. A second RP noted the subject was known to carry a gun. Although they did not see it today.

We had quite a few calls stacked up in the queue.

The responding officer was attached to another call when he said he would be en route shortly to check on the disturbance. The officer said he did not need a backing unit at this time. He would let me know later.

"Tonight is going to be a good night. I can feel it," Jon said.

He knew this would make me angry. Every time Jon feels good, the devil he made a deal with pops up to make my night a living hell.

"I hate you," I said. "It's already a full screen. I swear the day shift does not care if these calls hold all day. If we left calls like this for them in the morning, we'd be screamed at."

"I think we should leave them a ton of shit," Jon laughed. "I'd love to see them come for me."

"Yeah, but everyone is afraid of you." I re-evaluated my statement, "Except for me and maybe Carrie."

"You're afraid of me?" Jon stared.

"Ha. You wish."

I actually was afraid of him for the first year I worked there. Jon is a bit of a loose cannon. I would not talk to him if I didn't find his cantankerous demeanor so amusing.

He is a bit of a bitch.

"Ugh, now what?" My alert tones were going off, letting me know I had a priority onecall. [6]

I scanned the call. It was a DOA at the retirement home. This is a dual response with the fire department. It was an expected death, but we still sent an officer to document it and call the medical examiner's office if they didn't already have hospice on site. Most of the time, they do.

While handling the DOA, I kept an eye on the deputy going to a disturbance by himself. He pulled off to the side of the roadway to make a phone call regarding the first CFS he was attached to. He pulled over near the disturbance call. Therefore, I did not think much of it when he cleared himself in the CAD system from the first call and put himself "on scene" of the disturbance.

"98-year-old lady, I bet there's going to be a full investigation into her death," I chuckled loud enough for Jon to hear.

"Are you going to call homicide?" Jon asked.

"Ha. Yes."

Another call came in for the disturbance from a very intoxicated female. This time she said that the suspect had his gun. I looked at the call and saw that the deputy had been on the scene for about 2 minutes. I told her we had an officer on the scene and she should talk to him. I got on the radio to inform the officer to be advised that the suspect had apparently gotten his gun. He copied the transmission, and that was that.

"Looks like this drunk guy got his gun out anyway," I said.

---

[6] Priority 1 calls have an imminent threat of death or serious harm.

"You going to send a backing unit to that?" Audrey asked from the supervisor's desk.

"Yeah, I updated him, and he didn't seem too concerned. I'll get Sam 14 en route after I broadcast this other call," I said.

"Mary cars, report of a disturbance at the KFC on Weller. Customer upset over a refund, screaming and yelling, refusing to leave, no weapons."

As I was broadcasting that, I got an update on the disturbance call. We received another call from the neighbor who lived across the street from the disturbance. The RP advised he heard gunshots.

Fuck.

I was immediately worried about my officer.

I attempted to get his status on the radio, no answer. I tried again, no answer.

I put the radio on priority traffic and got units going that way—advising them that the unit on scene was not answering status checks.

Fuck.

"Sam 12, status." Still no answer. "Sam 12." "Your status."

"Sam 14, I'm about 2 mins out. I'm hearing gunshots from here."

Fuck.

Six more units went en route.

A few seconds later, Sam 12 came over the radio and advised he was on the scene.

Confused, I asked, "Sam 12, copy on scene. Your status?"

"I have one at gunpoint."

This kept the priority traffic status on, and the other units still incoming at code speeds.

"Sam 14, I'm with him. We're attempting to take one into custody. Keep the air held." Then, after another minute, I heard, "One in custody, open the air."

Relief, confusion, and anger washed over me. What just happened? I tried to understand the events in my head. Did he have a shootout with the suspect? Why didn't he respond to my first status checks?

As I have explained, dispatchers often go to the worst-case scenarios first.

"What in the hell just happened?" Audrey asked.

"I am so confused," I said.

I was still worried that I messed up bad. I wish I had started another unit right away. When you work with the city units and a gun comes out, you immediately send help. The county units are a bit laxer. Every country bumkin and yokel has a gun. If you send two units to a report of a man with a gun, they'll often give you sass and tell you to stand the backing unit down. 90% of the time, it's just a hunter or someone out doing target practice.

"Did you fuck up?" Jon asked with a half grin on his face.

Such an asshole.

"I don't know. Maybe?" I explained that it was just a drunk guy with a gun. At the time of the officer's arrival, he'd just gone to get it. No one was threatened with it, and no one had reported shots fired.

"It was also weird because he wasn't answering status after the tones went out. His first radio transmission said he was on the scene. But he'd already been there for a few mins," I said.

After Sam 12 took the suspect to jail, he stopped by the office to explain what happened. "I pulled over to make a call for the first CFS. I dispatched myself to the disturbance but didn't mean to mark myself on the scene. I was not actually there at that point. I didn't hear my status checks because I was listening to ensure I didn't hear gunshots as I rolled up to the scene."

"Didn't you hear the priority tones?" I asked, still trying to sort it in my head.

"I did, but I didn't realize they were for me. So I parked and walked up to the house to make contact with the suspect. In hindsight, I should not have done it because I wasn't sure if I was hearing gunshots," Sam 12 said. "With the tones on, I should have realized I wouldn't be able to broadcast if I needed assistance."

"Well, then, what happened?"

"As soon as the guy sees me, he pulls his gun out. He didn't point it at me, but he had it in his hand removed from the holster. That's when I drew my own weapon and pointed it at him. Once the guy saw I had my gun out, he realized what he did. He, thankfully, dropped his gun right away and went into custody willingly. Not a bad dude, just drunk and fucked up."

"What did you book him on?" I asked. Since he didn't draw his weapon at the officer, he technically had discretion over whether or not to arrest.

"I had to take him for unlawful discharge. The dude has a felony conviction, so he shouldn't have guns anyway. Plus, he was trashed. He was going to hurt someone," Sam 12 said. "He was super chill about it and understood he needed to sober up."

"Well, I'm glad you're ok."

"Yeah. I am really sorry. I should not have dispatched myself. I'm grateful that you got everyone to me so quickly. Sam 14 was there right as the guy was dropping his gun."

The officers understand how stressful our jobs can be when they don't follow procedures. How helpless we can feel when all we can do is be the calm voice in their heads.

For all the frustrations they may cause us, they really are our children, and we care deeply about their safety and well-being and want them to know we have their backs.

The relationship between officer and dispatcher is extraordinary, and I am thankful I get to do this for a living.

11

The Paradox Of Ignorance: Knowing Nothing Can Be A Gift

radio transmission
Dispatch: Engine 15, BLS response 1234 Main Street, Downtown quadrant for a lift assit.
Engine 15: En Route.
Dispatch: Engine 15 en route to 1234 Main Street. Your patient will be an 89-year-old male, non-injury lift assist.
Engine 15: Copy.
3 minutes later
Engine 15: Dispatch, show Engine 15 on scene at 1234 Main Street, uh, we're not able to locate the patient. Did they say where they would be?
Dispatch: That's the address that they gave.
Engine 15: Well, we are on scene here and unable to locate.
Dispatch: Did you try looking inside of the residence?
Engine 15: Oh…. We'll try that.

Firefighters are heroes.

They do a lot of grunt work that I am thankful every single day I do not have to deal with, smell, or touch. So don't get me wrong when I say sometimes, they can cause a great deal of unnecessary stressors to a dispatcher's work life. However, I try to be understanding and reasonably explain firefighter's lack of radio etiquette.

They do not get quite as many calls as law enforcement gets. Therefore they aren't as practiced.

They can have three to four people on a rig, and sometimes they share radio duties. Therefore, firefighters are not as individually practiced.

Fire trucks are noisy. Perhaps they just misheard me?

At the end of the day, sometimes the term "hose-draggers" describes my firefighters.[1]

September 13TH, 2019 – 8 Hour Shift

I had no idea how common of an occurrence vehicle fires actually were until I started working here," I said.

"Oh yeah, we see quite a few," Carries said.

"I know, but I don't know anyone whose car was on fire in my personal life. They are weirdly common, and I figured I would have some personal experience with it," I said.

"You don't?" Carrie asked. "My husband's car went up in flames one night in the '90s. Thankfully, no one was driving it. It was just parked in the driveway. They thought it was arson at first but think it's more likely to have been some sort of critter got up in the manifold and somehow connected the wrong wires, and all it takes is a spark."

"That's crazy. Did you at least get an insurance payout for the vehicle?"

"I think so," Carrie said. "That was a long time ago."

Carrie has not only been around the Communication Center for a very long time but she's also been on the planet

---

[1] Or pipe men, smoke eaters, ladder monkeys, hose jockey, you get the idea.

for a very long time. I swear she has a story for everything. I really appreciate her stories, and it seems like she's been through everything. Kids, divorce, a second husband dying of cancer, and a car fire.

Earlier in the shift, I had a report of a two-vehicle collision, non-injury, and heavy front-end damage. It seemed routine. The RP reported that one vehicle was smoking. When this is reported, the RP often sees the dust settling from the airbag deployment. However, this time, the vehicle really was smoking and sparked up. It went fully enflamed. I updated the units already en route.

"Uhh, copy dispatch. The vehicle is now up in flames. Go ahead and send us one more Engine."

"Received." I dispatched another unit.

"Engine 14 en route. Copy other units as well. Did we get a description of the vehicle that's on fire?"

"Affirm. 4 wheels, heavy front-end damage, fire and smoke coming out of the front of it. Can't miss it."

"Uhhh, copy."

"Keep it professional, Jackson," Audrey yelled.

"But they're so dumb," I whined back.

Audrey glared. She knows I mean no harm and probably thinks I'm funny. But since she's the boss, she has to reprimand me. We both understand the system.

"I won't do it again," I lied.

After work, I met with my dear friend, Fernanda, for dinner and drinks. Fernanda had been a dispatcher in the past for a couple of years. She got to the point. Like countless others, she did not want to deal with the Communication

Center's drama and the trauma of the job itself. I applaud her for sticking out the two years that she did.

I recounted the story of the dumb firefighter who wanted a description of the vehicle on fire.

"Ha. I've heard a fire dispatcher say something similar before. It was, 'Yes, we got a description. *It's a bright red car due to the flames*, so you're definitely not alone in that," we laughed. "You shouldn't have gotten in trouble for that. That's dumb."

"I technically just got told to keep it professional. I didn't actually get in trouble for anything," I said.

"That's good. I know how quick they are to write someone up. Especially if Bunny is still working there."

Fernanda had all the same experiences with particular supervisors that I did. There have been several promotions since she worked there, but she technically knew everyone. I love having a friend like Fernanda who truly understands me.

"I was talking to Carrie afterward about how shocked I was at how many vehicle fires there are. It almost makes me scared to drive," I said. "Until hearing her personal story of a car fire, I did not know a single person who had a car fire, and that kind of shocks me."

"Uh… me," Fernanda said.

"What?" I asked, "You've had a vehicle fire before?"

"Yeah. Did I not tell you this story?"

"Not that I recall," I set my drink down and put my hands under my chin, ready for a great story.

"It was one of my first cars. After the "69 Volkswagen Beetle, I bought a red 80s something Ford Tempo. It was everything 17-year-old me could have dreamed of, especially after driving the bug where nothing worked. I went to a party up in the middle of nowhere. I parked in someone's hay field. We were all underage, so we'd throw these big parties on my friend's farm. Anyway, the fire started in the engine and was fully engulfed fast." She expanded her hands out to show the motion of the flames spreading out.

"Wow, I don't think you've ever told me that story," I said.

"I feel like I have," Fernanda said.

"I think I would have remembered."

"Well, anyway, it was a nightmare because I lost my purse, new leather jacket, and some of my favorite CDs."

I interrupted, "CDs? In a 1980s? Also, did you have CDs in high school?" I love reminding her that she's older than me. I take advantage of this every chance I get. She's only a month and a week older, but I make sure she never forgets. Including mentioning it here, where I know she'll read it.

"Shut up! We definitely had CDs when *we* were *both* in high school. At the *same* time, since *we* graduated the *same* year. Anyway, I was working at Best Buy at the time, and I got a cheap car CD player with my discount, and my friend installed it for me," she said. "It was a holiday weekend, and I was supposed to work the next day. I had requested the day off, and it got declined. So I called my boss and told her what happened and that there was no way I could make it to work as I was stuck ninety miles away for another day until I could get a ride back home. She totally didn't believe me until I showed her the pictures later."

"Oh my god, do you still have the pictures?" I asked.

"Probably. Somewhere. I don't know where though," she said.

"Well, I want to see them when you find them." As of me writing this, I have still never seen the photos. What is that about, Fernanda[2]?

October 5TH, 2018 – 12 Hour Shift

Traffic collisions are an everyday event. It would be a strange day if I went home without handling a traffic collision. Since they are routine events, one would think it would be difficult for someone dealing with such a familiar situation to mess it up. Right?

Send in the clowns!

We got a report of a three-car pileup on the main highway in and out of town. At that particular part of the road, it is a two-lane highway. One northbound lane and one southbound lane. It is flat, and they have large shoulders on both sides, surrounded by a heavily wooded area. The person reporting the collision was not involved and drove by the scene. The firetruck that I had en route to the scene gets on the radio and attempts to get clarification on the location of the collision.

I told him what I knew, "The RP was a passerby, stated he was headed northbound on the highway between milepost 9 and 10. Three vehicles to the side of the road – white pickup

---

[2] I told her about this story. She said she wanted a footnote about how I've now seen the photos. As of four weeks to publication, I still haven't seen them.

truck versus a black passenger car versus another black passenger car."

"And which side of the freeway is this on?" the engine asked.

"The caller was headed northbound and stated it was on the side of the highway," I repeated exactly what I knew.

"Right, but the RP was headed northbound. Did he say the collision was also in the northbound lane?"

"He did not specify," I said.

"Ok, can you call the RP back and find out if the collision was on the east side of the highway or the west side?"

Now, I know some of you might argue that for these types of incidences, the fire truck positions itself to block the roadway to provide safety and awareness to other drivers on the highway, so they would need to know east or west to enter the scene correctly and place the engine. You would be correct. That is an important factor when determining the location on LARS,[3] such as an interstate where the northbound onramp for a location might be 1-2 miles south of a collision. However, in this case, we had one engine responding and only one way to the scene, and it is a tiny highway; therefore, the east side or west side is irrelevant.

"I hate working fire radio," I said.

Laura, working on the police radio, was a computer away from me.

"What are they doing now?" Laura asked.

---

[3] Limited Access Roadways

"They're going to that collision where you have Charlie 22 en route. They want to know if the collision is on the east or west side of the roadway," I said.

"What difference does it make on that road?" Laura asked.

"Exactly my point. It's also a minor injury fender-bender. It's not like we have CPR in progress."

I knew she would understand. I grabbed my phone and started to dial back to the original RP. The engine got on the scene of the collision before I even got to the second ring of the callback, and I wish I could say it's a rare occurrence.

But it's not.

"Oh wow, surprise, surprise. They found the collision without my help," I said.

"You should probably play the lottery with that kind of luck," Laura said.

We chuckled at the ridiculousness of it all.

"Copy that."

"They must be a special crew today. The officers are even annoyed by them." Laura was laughing.

"Oh, what's going on?" I pulled up the call to read any updated notes.

"She said that they've come on the scene and established command, and now my officer has to wait to do her investigation until they're done playing. Those are her words, not mine," Laura said.

"Playing?" I laughed and shook my head, "They're probably cutting the batteries *just in case.*"

"Right? They're probably putting everyone involved into a C-spine collar *just in case,*" Laura said.

"They are probably recommending flight for life on everyone, *just in case.*"

If you haven't seen the YouTube cartoon comedy "Highway Patrol" it's worth a view. Particularly episode 5. It's an exaggeration but extremely accurate. Don't believe me? Look at the comment section.

"Do you have to work fire radio all night or just for your overtime portion?" Laura asked.

"All freakin' night," I said. "Hopefully, it'll be a quiet night."

"You just jinxed yourself."

"Oh no... I just used the Q word. I will regret that."

And I did.

The evening continued reasonably routine. A bump and bruise here, a cut hand over there, chest pains, and another minor collision. The small collision was in another area and was not as dramatic.

A priority one fire call comes up on my screen. I read it.

RP states neighbor's garage is smoking, hearing crackling noises, thinks possible structure fire. Not seeing flames.

"This could be interesting," I said as I sent out the tones. "Engine 13, Engine 17, possible residential structure fire, 7249 10 Avenue. Neighbor seeing smoke and crackling noises. No visible flames."

"Show us en route," Engine 17 said.

RP now seeing flames and says the house is definitely involved as well. Also, seeing possible fireworks exploding.

"Uh, that's different." I stepped on my pedal and broadcasted, "Engine 13, 17, be advised, the caller states fire has spread to the house. The caller now sees flames and possible fireworks. I'm going to upgrade to a full response."

"Engine 17 copies."

I toned out a full structure response, which included another engine, a medic unit, an ambulance, and a battalion che. I also advised the police dispatcher to let her know they may be needed for traffic control.

"Engine 17 to dispatch, we are on the scene of a 2 story, wood frame single family structure mostly involved with activity on the Alpha and Delta sides now and—" the transmission cut out. "Uh, dispatch, we have some popping noises. Uh—we're getting out of here. I think someone is shooting."

"Copy, possible shots fired on the scene of the structure fire. All incoming units stand down for now. We will be getting a police response. Once again, all units stand down." I glanced at Laura.

She had overheard most of it and upgraded her response to the scene. "Do we have any description of a shooter? Location? Anything?" Laura asked all the right questions.

I had none of the answers yet.

"Let me make sure they're all copying that we're standing down, and I'll see if I can get more out of Engine 17."

"Good plan."

"Once again, we need all fire units to stand down. Possible active shooter on the fire scene, all units roll call to copy standing down," I broadcasted. "Engine 17, confirm you are leaving the scene."

"Affirm, we've left."

"Engine 13, verify you copy."

"Affirm. Copy. We never got on scene."

"Medic 17, verify you copy."

"Medic 17, affirmative. Never on scene."

"Aid 13, verify you copy."

"Affirmative. A13 is back in quarters."

"Battalion Chief 17, verify you copy?"

Nothing.

"Battalion Chief 17, verify you copy to stand down. Active shooter situation on the structure fire scene."

Nothing.

"Battalion Chief 17. Hear radio." I was not doing well at this point. "Battalion Chief 17. Hear radio."

"I have his personal cell. I'm going to call him," Audrey said from the supervisor's desk. Thank god she always pays attention to the big stuff.[4]

"Battalion Chief 17. Hear radio." Nothing. "Medic 17, is he still at the fire station?"

"We will be back in two minutes and will advise."

"Copy." I had a brief moment, "Engine 17, can you tell us anything about the active shooter."

---

[4] This sums up a supervisors job function. Unfortunately, a lot of them are reactive and not proactive when you need them to be.

"Engine 17, we did not get a good look. We were sizing up the structure and heard the popping. We saw what looked to be a long gun poking out of one of the windows. Possibly a male suspect shooting towards us."

"Copy, long gun. Possibly a male suspect. Can you tell what side of the house that was?" I asked.

"Affirm. This would be from the alpha side."

"Were any of your crew injured, or your rig hit?"

"Negative on crew injuries. We will pull over here in a minute to inspect our rig."

"Copy Engine 17. Please advise immediately on any damage." I updated Laura with the shooter information. In the middle of me giving her the details, I get interrupted.

"Battalion Chief 17 is fine. He's having radio issues. He copied all the transmissions and then tried to call 911 to let us know that he was ok. However, the 911 lines got backed up, and he couldn't get through. He's going to stage at the Kroger's on 14 Ave and wants his units to also stage there with him," Audrey said, phone still by her cheek.

I sighed in relief and returned to work, "Engine 13, Medic 17, Aid 13, Battalion Chief is ok. The radio in his rig stopped working. Chief will be staging at Kroger's on 14 Ave and requests you all join him there."

After they all copied, I checked back in with Engine 17. "Do you have any updates for me, Engine 17?"

"We have no damage here. We will join the other units at Kroger's."

"Copy," I said.

That could have been so much worse.

Matthew Johnson wanted to end his life that day. He was laid off from his high-paying job, his wife left him and took the kids, he was unable to pay his bills, and the house was going into foreclosure.

Matthew went to Lowe's, a 76 gas station, and a fireworks stand that morning. He went to work on a plan. The bank wanted to take his house, so he wouldn't leave a house for them to take. He set up fireworks all around the house. He poured a trail of gasoline that ran from one end of the fireworks to the other. The investigation team presumed the plan was to start a fire at one end of the home and have it work to the garage, where he would have a stand-off with police, possibly with a suicide-by-cop finality.

Something went wrong with the plan, and some combustibles ignited in the garage first. Based on where Matthew's stockpile was located, he moved from the garage to the laundry room area. When the first engine arrived at the scene, he shot at them, and they left.

By the time the officer arrived, Matthew had to move again. The laundry room already caught on fire. Instead of moving deeper into the house, already rigged to go up in flames, his only option was to move back into the garage. Officers could not get very close to the structure because they did not know where the shooter was, and the flames were uncontrolled.

Officers did not believe that the suspect could still be in the house with the amount of fire going on. However, they could not rule it out either. After a perimeter was cleared, a nearby incident command was created, and the fire apparatuses moved in. Still unable to work on the structure fire, they did their best to contain it to the house and garage.

After enough time passed, there was no sign of any shooter in the vicinity, and all neighbor's homes were checked. Police allowed the firefighters in with escorts to put out the burning house. Despite it being burned down to its frames at this point.

Matthew was located inside the trunk of his vehicle, which was parked inside the garage. Investigators speculate that Matthew must have seen the writing on the wall of his failed plans. He took cover inside his vehicle in what he must have thought was a safe space.

As we have previously discussed, vehicles are very flammable.[5]

November 22ND, 2019 – 12 Hour Shift

A laugh rang out from Melanie, who was manning the fire radio. She even snorted a little. "That's amazing."

"What is going on?" I asked.

"Oh my gosh. I have to get Robert over here," she typed a message to Robert through the CAD system.

"What's up?" Robert asked.

"Tell me about that buzzing call you just took," Melanie said.

"Oh, the one on Rose Street?" Robert asked.

---

[5] Unverified, but I heard that the vehicle was a hotrod. I had to snake this in. Sorry, not sorry.

"Yeah."

"Ok, well, a woman called, and she said she heard an electrical-sounding buzz in the walls. No smoke, no visible flames. Why? Did we find out what it was?"

"Oh, yeah," Melanie started giggling again. "Listen to this." Melanie played back the radio transmissions from a few minutes earlier. "Engine 18, report of a possible electrical malfunction in the wall at 7845 Rose Street. RP reported hearing a buzzing sound inside the wall. No smoke. No flames."

"Copy, show us en route."

"Engine 18 on scene of a one-story wood framed structure, no flames or smoke seen from the outside. Making contact."

"Copy, no smoke. No flames. One-story wood framed structure." We always repeat for brevity on structure fire calls. She fast-forwarded the recording by a few minutes.

"Engine 18, we are clear here. Problem was identified."

"Copy. Clear on scene," Melanie broadcasted.

"Uh, Engine 18, what was the problem you identified," a man's voice came across on the radio.

"Engine 18, repeat?"

"Engine 18, this is Chief 18. What was the problem you identified?"

"Engine 18, the buzzing sound was a—uh—personal massager that got knocked behind the dresser and buzzed into the wall."

"Copy that," Chief 18 said.

We all exploded into laughter.

"That is amazing," Robert said.

"That's exactly what I said," Melanie giggled through it. We all were making buzzing sounds and replaying the scene with each other.

"Shhhhh," said a familiar voice. It was Mike The Dick, coming to destroy the vibe. "You're being too loud. We can't hear the other frequencies."

"Sorry," Melanie said. She tried to explain what had happened and why it was so funny, but he didn't care. Instead, he cut her off and instructed Robert to return to his call-taking spot.

Mike The Dick is a buzz-kill, but I guess he was right. We did get a little loud.

"Audrey would have thought it was hilarious," I whispered to Melanie after Mike The Dick returned to his supervisor's desk.

"I mean, we *were* being a little loud." Melanie also understood.

"Yeah, but I think she would have been nicer about it."

"Obviously."

I eventually told Audrey about the dildo incident, and she did, in fact, find it hilarious. I told her about Mike The Dick. Audrey said she could understand why we were loud. I asked her if he wrote anything about it in our personnel files because he would do that.

He didn't.

He wasn't as angry about it as he seemed to be.[6]

---

[6] He probably needs his own personal massager.

I strive for professionalism, even if I enjoy having a little bit of fun that sometimes toes the line. Later when my shift ended, I had to stay over in a call-taking position.

This call made me toe that line again.

We are required to have medical training to take medical calls and give pre-arrival advice and instruction. Mostly though, we read from a script that was designed by medical professionals. Not every medical situation can be coded into a quick guide. If it was, that quick guide would be longer than the bible.

"What are you reporting?" I asked.

"My mother is having a seizure," said a frantic woman.

"Does she have a seizure disorder?" I asked.

"Yes. She is epileptic but hasn't had a full-blown seizure in a long time. She manages it with her meds."

"Alright, is she still actively seizing?" I asked.

"No, I don't think so."

"Ok, well, as she's coming out of it, monitor her breathing." I'm typing all of this information into the CFS and have had a call started since she gave me her address.

"I don't think she's breathing," the woman said. Panic resurfacing.

"When someone returns from seizing, it can take a bit and be tough to tell if they're breathing. So just make sure there are no obstructions," I said.

"It looks like she's choking."

"What is she choking on?" I asked. "Can you see?"

"Well, my fingers are in her mouth," she said.

I snorted a little bit.

This is where you'll see the real medical training come into play here.

"Uhm, let's go ahead and take your fingers out of her mouth. Is she breathing ok?"

"Yeah."

That is a solid way to lose a finger. I really wanted to tell her that.

I didn't.

I am a professional.

March 19TH, 2014 – 8 Hour Shift

One would think a firefighter's job on a structure fire is straightforward. They put the wet stuff on the hot stuff. It's not exactly rocket science.

If you remember, in chapter one, we discussed how responses changed after September 11th, 2001. The federal government, through a national program called NIMS (National Incident Management System), is housed under FEMA (Federal Emergency Management Agency). They required all fire agencies to follow a formulated incident command system on every call. The beauty of this system is that it can be as large or as small as the incident itself.

On the one hand, it simplifies the scene because we have a pattern that molds to every situation. It does not matter if the response includes multiple ambulances, fire trucks, and police. Command is still established, and everything is delegated down from there. The first unit on the scene establishes

Command. Once they get on the scene, Command is transferred to a higher-ranking official, such as a Duty Chief. The Duty Chief then delegates different units into many other parts, Safety Coordinator, Public Information Officer, Operations, Planning, Logistics, Finance, and Administration.

Under the Operations Officer, active units are working the scene, such as the police, paramedics, firefighters, etc. The Operations Officers are responsible for keeping track of where and what they are doing. They can also form Strike Teams, which are groups of like apparatuses. For instance, if we had multiple groups of paramedics, a Strike Team Leader would be established, and they would be responsible for the EMTs and paramedics working under them.

Strike Team Leader reports to the Operations Officer and the Operations Officer Reports to Command. Everyone is accountable for what they are doing. Everyone has a job and knows what their job entails. It makes it easy to fold in units that do not typically work together. On larger incidents, mutual aid may be requested from a nearby county. These units get on scene, are immediately given a place within the incident command system, and know exactly their role and where they exist on the chain of Command.

Even with the Command established, some units forget how Command is supposed to go. Technically, the request is ignored if an individual unit speaks to dispatch out of turn and they are not Command. They are required to make the request on the operational channel to Command. However, it does not always go this way. Despite being highly versed in incident command, firefighters often forget the procedures. It can be incredibly frustrating.

"Working fire radio again, eh Jackson?" Jon asked with a smile on his face.

"Yes, sir, and I am happy about it," I lied. I wouldn't give him the satisfaction of getting on my nerves today. "I just finished my NIMS training and feel more confident on the firefighter channel."

He walked away without further incident. I avoided Jon's sass while he walked around looking for another target. He looked at Jose, the newest call-taker, as he walked by.

Target acquired.

"I heard you messed up pretty good on that call on the south end?" Jon asked Jose.

"Oh? What call?" Jose asked with terror in his eyes.

"Oh. Management hasn't talked to you yet?" Jon grasped at his chest. Wow. What a dick.

"Uh, no." Jose looked pale. "Do you know what I did wrong?"

"I probably shouldn't say." Jon walked away.

"Don't worry, Jon likes to stir the pot. You probably didn't do anything. He just likes to keep everyone scared," I assured Jose.

I mean, I don't know Jose all that well.

Maybe he did mess up a call.

"That's an insulting thing to do," Jose said.

"It really is." I wasn't going to try to defend him at all. Jon is an asshole.

I approached the fire dispatch terminal to confront Jon and stand up for Jose. Jon had his back to me. He was talking to Carrie.

"Did you know we've been working together for almost 19 years?" Carrie said to Jon.

"Yeah, I'm basically like a brother at this point, but a brother that thinks you're hot. So it's a bizarre relationship," Jon said.

I decided I wanted no part of that conversation and walked away. Jose could fight his own battles.

A traffic collision came in. It was a gnarly head-on, and the second vehicle went off the side of the highway and rolled over a few times. Definitely going to be some injuries. I tone out a full collision response; two engines, a medic, and an aid car. I let Jon know to send the police to take the report.

The first engine gets on the scene and sets up Highway 10 command. Perfect. The aid crew and medic units get on the scene with no problems. The second engine gets on the scene and takes over Command. Again, no problems.

"Highway 10 command to radio, can we get a law enforcement response for traffic control?" It was the first annoying question of the incident.

How fun.

"They've been advised, and I show two units en route," I said.

The police officers do this too. If they are first on the scene, they will ask if we have toned out for aid. I always think, *No, sugar, we thought you were Superman and could handle it all.*

After the initial size-up, we finally understand what we are looking at. We have five patients, three green, one yellow, one red.[7] Not bad, all things considered. Fire starts patient care, and *someone* requests a helicopter for flight-for-life. They did not specify that they were Command, but I get it. It was a critical incident, so I got a helicopter started. I assumed it was Highway 10 Command who had requested it. I confirmed the launch, the landing zone prepped, and ETA relayed.

"Highway 10 Command, Airlift ETA of 16 minutes, landing zone will be the airfield," I advised.

"Highway 10 Command to radio, cancel Airlift."

That is never a good sign.

"Copy. Canceling Airlift," I confirmed. I called back Airlift and told them to stand down. Usually, this means that the critical patient did not make it. They need to be able to prove ROSC – Return of Spontaneous Circulation. This means either a pulse, breathing, moving, or measurable blood pressure to get them on an Airlift to a trauma hospital.

Five more minutes pass by, and I hear over the radio again, "Radio, do we have an ETA for Airlift?"

"Airlift was canceled at 13:42 by Highway 10 Command," I confirmed.

"Negative, continue Airlift," said the voice. Semi-untrusting, I did as instructed, and I called Airlift back. The dispatcher for Airlift was equally as confused, but we decided that they must have achieved some sort of ROSC and hurray

---

[7] Green = good; Yellow = ehhh; Red = needs a medic; Black is meeting Jesus.

for that patient. Once again, I got the launch, landing zone, and ETA confirmed.

"Highway 10 Command, Airlift ETA of 15 minutes, landing zone will be the airfield," I advised again.

"Highway 10 Command to dispatch. Once again! That is a NEGATIVE on Airlift. Cancel Airlift." This was a very gruff incident commander.

"Copy. Canceling Airlift," I repeated loudly. Then, I called back to the airlift dispatcher; she was very understanding and friendly about the situation.

Another two or three minutes passed, and a familiar voice came over the radio again, "Radio, can we get an updated ETA on Airlift?"

"Negative. Airlift has been stood down by Highway 10 Command," I said clearly and concisely.

"Negative. We need a launch of Airlift," the voice said.

"Negative. If an Airlift launch is needed, it must come from Highway 10 Command." I had fallen for this twice now. I was not going to fall for this folly again.

Silence.

Part of our job is to control the situation. If it had been a request for a tow truck from a random voice, I would have told him to refer to the incident command right away. However, the severity and time-sensitivity of the situation made me decide to launch the helicopter despite not verifying that the request came from Command. The critical patient on the side of the roadway needing trauma care outweighed my need to be correct.

Later I would have to talk to the Duty Chief about this incident. Apparently, the first engine still felt like they had Command even though it had been taken over by the second engine. The decision had been made that the critical care patient was going to be transported to the hospital via ambulance as they had stabilized them enough for the more extended transport. The Duty Chief stood by my decision and thanked me for my efforts.

Unfortunately, Jon sucked me in, and I asked, "Did Jose actually mess up a call, or were you just messing with him?"

"He messed up a call," Jon said without missing a beat.

"Oh really? That's not good. I'm tired of the constant turnover causing all of this overtime. Jose seemed like he was doing a good enough job. But I never work with him," I said.

"How do you know I'm not messing with you now?" Jon asked quite astutely.

"God, I hate you."

February 10ᵀᴴ, 2015 – 12 Hour Shift

Using fancy medical terminology on the air, as if I know what I am talking about, is one of my favorite things to do while dispatching medical emergencies. For example, the patient is experiencing a syncopal episode, fasciculation in the fourth vertebra, and is on warfarin for a previous cardiovascular accident. In layman's terms – the patient has a back spasm, is about to pass out, and is taking medications for a stroke. It sounds so much fancier the other way, and it is the little things that bring me joy.

Firefighters also enjoy sounding fancier than they are too. It almost got me into trouble with the Fire Chief once.

We got a report of a gasoline spill on a roadway. The RP had estimated it to be between 10-15 gallons worth. For this kind of incident, I send out a HAZMAT (Hazardous Materials) response, which consists of two engines and an air unit. An air unit looks like an ambulance but is packed with O2 containers to assist firefighters in changing their tanks.

The first engine gets on the scene, creates the incident command, and confirms what the original RP reported. Command requests that all incoming units continue in. The air unit driver is an older woman with a funny robotic voice. She talks very slowly and over-enunciates each word. "Air. Three-One. On. The. Scene."

"Copy, Air 31 on scene," I said quickly. After about ten minutes on scene, I get another transmission from Air 31.

"Air. Three-One. To. Dispatch," very slowly.

"Go ahead"

"Air. Three-One," in case I forgot, "Requesting. An. Additional. Response. To. Scene. Also," this signifies that there is more to say.

"Go ahead."

"Air-Three-One," Really? "Requesting. The. Additional. Responder. Bring. Magic. Dirt."

I had no idea what magic dirt was. I was laughing with my partner about the entire transmission. These requests came from outside of Incident Command. But it was a small request, and I decided to follow through rather than argue. I replied through my laughter, "Received."

I toned out the next available unit, as requested. It was a ladder truck, and I included the request for *magic dirt*. The ladder truck got on the radio before they went en route.

"Dispatch from Ladder 10, confirm the request for magic dirt?" he sounded confused.

"Affirmative, the request was for Magic Dirt," I was trying to hold back the giggles.

"Ladder 10 to Air 31, confirm your request."

Ha! They had no idea what she was talking about.

"Air-Three-One. To. Ladder. 10. Go. Ahead."

Oh, good lord.

"Ladder 10, confirm your request for magic dirt."

"Air-Three-One. That. Is. Affirmative. Magic. Dirt," she said confidently.

"Can you advise what Magic Dirt is?"

"Air-Three-One. The. Absorbent. Material."

I am laughing so hard.

"Received," stated the ladder unit. "Radio, show Ladder 10 en route with eight packages of absorbent material."

With tears streaming down my face, trying to choke back the laughter, I barely eked out, "Received." Laughing on the radio is unacceptable, and apparently, the Fire Chief was not in the mood for humor. So I got a slap on the wrist for that one.

12

All Those Things You Said Keep Running Through My Dumb My Thick Head

I told you we must keep celebrities' anonymity when they call 911, but my lawyer approved this one, enjoy.

Dispatch: 911, Where is your emergency?

Female Caller: This is Nicki Minaj, and I am reporting a theft.

Dispatch: Ok, hello, Nicki. When did this occur?

Nicki Minaj: Oh, it's an ongoing issue. Chris Brown stole $5000 from my record label.

Dispatch: Ok, is he there now?

Nicki Minaj: Hells no, I would beat his ass!

Dispatch: Ok, well, Nicki Minaj, this is a civil matter between you, Chris Brown, and the record label. There's not really anything the police will be able to do right now.

Nicki Minaj: Chris Brown is such an ASSHOLE! If he was here right now, I would BEAT HIS ASS!

Dispatch: I know Nicki Minaj, a lot of people feel that way, but again, you should probably call your lawyer and the record label, ok?

Nicki Minaj: Well, how do I get my $5000 back?

Dispatch: Again, you have to call your lawyer.

Nicki Minaj: Alright, thank you.

You were talking to Nicki Minaj, eh?" Terrance asked.

"I am very confident that I was," I smiled. "I'm pretty sure I've talked to her before, but last time she wasn't Nicki Minaj."

"Oh? Who was she last time?" Terrance asked.

"She was Beyoncé for me a few weeks ago," Melanie said.

"That's right, she *was* Beyoncé. I think she was mad at Solange or something. She's always upset with someone when she is one of her famous personalities." I noted.

"Do we even know what her real name is?" Terrance asked.

"Yeah, it's in the history tab. I can't remember off-hand. You just kind of step into the delusion, give her something else to focus on, and she's harmless," I said. "If you try to talk her out of the delusion, she'll dig in deeper, and you'll struggle."

"Oh, for sure." Terrance is a very experienced call-taker. I don't need to remind him. "Can you imagine if the real Nicki Minaj actually called, though, and we just tossed her aside thinking she was just a person with a mental health issue?"

"Honestly, if Nicki Minaj called in our town, I would for sure write her off as a crazy person and not think twice about it."

We all laughed because it was true.

When an actual famous person called in, I didn't believe them until I googled it.[1]

June 24TH, 2016 – 8 Hour Shift

---

[1] Still not sorry.

People call 911 for all sorts of inappropriate reasons. I don't fault them if it is in earnest and they're unsure who to call. For instance, an old lady with a raccoon running around her house. Is it appropriate for the 911 line?

No.

Do I fault her for calling us?

Absolutely not. Sometimes people need to be told what to do. I'm always happy to let them know they need to call an exterminator. I don't get upset when they turn ugly or mad that we won't solve their inconvenience.

I'm happy to listen to that unfold.

However, I can't say the same for Jon.

"What are you reporting exactly?" Jon asked. He has a particular tone when he starts to get annoyed with a caller. I could be in the middle of a conversation with someone, and I will drop everything to listen in. "Uh-huh, but I'm still not hearing what you are reporting."

"Oh man, here we go," I said, making eye contact with Laura. I can't suppress the grin.

"Ok, are you trying to report that the power is out in your building?" Jon asked.

I picked up the line to listen in.

"Yeah. It's dark here, and I can't see anything," the male caller said. He sounded like he could be elderly, but it wasn't overtly obvious. He may have been intoxicated. No immediate clues to anything based on the one sentence I heard.

"Ok, well, you need to call the power company if the power is out," Jon said calmly.

"It's dark in here," the man said.

"Ok, and what are you expecting the police to be able to do about that?" Jon knows we're all listening now. I think he's trying to be good.

"They should come and fix it."

"Well, that's not what the police do. They do not have master's degrees in electrical engineering," Jon said.

"Well, then send the fire department. They should be able to do something," the man said.

This man is just being difficult. He's not intoxicated, demented, or any other justifiable issue to trigger our empathy. I would wager that Jon is about two questions from being set off.

"No. That is not within their scope of responsibilities. So, once again, the most appropriate agency to handle your power outage would be your power company," Jon said curtly.

"Well, can't you call them?"

"Absolutely not. One, I don't know who you use as your power company. Two, we only send police, fire, or medics," Jon said.

"I don't understand why you can't do it. It's your job."

Oh shit. Here we go.

"It is absolutely not my job to make these calls for you. My job is to assist people who are having in-progress, life-threatening emergencies. Something I am now unable to do because I'm sitting here trying to get you to understand simple concepts. I need to answer the 911 lines for people with actual emergencies," Jon said.

"You can't hang up on me."

"Watch me." Jon disconnected the phone.[2]

235

I had to hang up quickly, or the man would be transferred to me. The best thing about Jon is that he immediately lets these things go.

Jon took another call. The person fell and needed a lift assist. He was professional, empathetic, and kind. Jon isn't a complete monster. He just has the inability to filter his thoughts when people call with nonsense.

Frustration is felt whenever we receive calls from someone like Mr. Power Outage. Especially the extremely entitled who feel their mild inconveniences are more critical than other people's emergencies. For example, I have had callers upset that the police haven't come to issue a parking ticket to a vehicle parked in the wrong direction because it's visually unappealing. They remain upset and indignant even after I explain that the police are delayed because of a shooting.

I would like to ask them, "Are you so insensitive that you think your parking complaint is more important than the guy who might die because he was an innocent bystander in a drive-by shooting?" But instead, I just keep with, "I apologize for the delay. We will get out there as soon as possible."

November 4TH, 2018 – 12 Hour Shift

Oh my god, you will never believe what I just had to deal with," Laura said.

"I bet I will believe it, but go ahead anyway," Carrie said.

---

[2] We absolutely can and will hang up if you don't have a legitimate emergency and want to be disrespectful instead.

"This woman called because she wanted the police to come to a restaurant and force them to make her dinner."

"Uh, what?" I asked.

"She walked in about twenty minutes before closing with a group of eight people and wanted to get a table. The restaurant, understandably, explains that they are unable to accommodate a group of that size since they are closing soon," Laura said. "She gets upset and demands to speak to a manager. The manager supported their worker's decision and apologized to the woman and advised them that they would still be unable to seat them."

"Let me guess, her name was Karen?" I asked.

"Might as well have been. She called 911 and demanded I send the police to deal with the unreasonable manager. I told her that I would not be sending the police. But, of course, that doesn't go over well, and she continues to yell at me and explain it all over again as if I'm the idiot. I interrupt her and attempt to make her see reason. *What do you expect the police to do?* And she says *they need to come here and force them to make us our dinner.* I told her that we would not be doing that," Laura said. She held an all too familiar piece of paper in her hand.[3]

"Now, she wants to speak to your supervisor?" Carrie asked.

Laura lifted the paper up so it was more visible.

"Yep." Laura handed Audrey the form. Audrey looked it over and chuckled.

---

[3] Furthermore, would you want to eat a dinner prepared by a kitchen full of people who hate you?

"I'm going to let her cool down a bit before I call her back," Audrey said. She placed the request in the inbox.

"Do you switch to radio soon?" I asked.

"No. I'm doing an all-nighter so that the new transfer, Travis, can get some radio time," Laura said.

"That's nice of you," Carrie said.

"Well, we need more people who are radio trained, so we stop getting hammered with all of this overtime," Laura said.

"You can be nice and self-absorbed, I think," I giggled.

Carrie shook her head and looked back to her screen. "Well, if you get overwhelmed on phones and need a break, I'll trade you for a bit."

"Thank you, but I'll be fine," Laura said, returning to her seat.

Looking at my dispatch screen, I watched a new call coming in. It left me confused. It looked like the caller wanted to turn himself in for a warrant. Not completely unheard of, but we generally do not put calls in for that kind of thing. They can go directly to the courthouse or the jail. We don't need to send a police officer to their house. Robbie, a new guy, entered the call.

Ah, that explains it.

I decided to handle the call myself. I picked up the phone, called the RP back, and asked what they were trying to do. The RP stated they wanted to find out *if* they had a warrant. I explained we don't run people over the phone and directed him to the correct place. I messaged Robbie and let him know that we don't need to put in a call. I deleted the call. No harm, no foul.

Other dispatchers are not so generous. I have witnessed some of my more tenured colleagues lay into some of these newbies over the simplest of errors. Our actions have serious real-world consequences. While I understand the seriousness of what we do, I still don't believe in yelling at new people while they're learning. It's so common in the dispatch centers that there is a phrase for it, *eating our young*. I first heard that phrase when I went to Telecommunicator school, a required piece of training in our state.

The instructor warned us that it was common in the dispatch center. One of the women in my class said that she felt prepared because she had experienced hazing in the military when she enlisted. I was flabbergasted. Thankfully, the instructor renounced this practice, gave us some tips and tricks to avoid falling victim to *being eaten*, and encouraged us to always remember this moment and be kind to the new people who follow us.

I haven't forgotten.

February 11TH, 2015 – 12 Hour Shift

Morale in the communication center hit a low point this winter. Generally speaking, the morale of a comm center is a rollercoaster. Many factors contribute to this, but nothing kills like a lousy supervisor. In the winter of 2015, we were introduced to the new hire, Becky. Upper management had decided to hire a lateral supervisor instead of promoting from within since the last few internal promotions did not go so well.

Nothing could have prepared us for Becky. Becky reminded me of a short guy in a big truck overcompensating an issue for no one but themselves. She must have felt that she had to prove herself as a new supervisor, but instead of being a leader, she barreled through and tried to command us to do her bidding. Even if it broke our internal policies.

"Hey, what's up?" Kelly asked at the supervisor's desk.

"You need to hold on a second," Becky raised her index finger.

I was nearby and overheard this entire interaction.

"Ok. Sorry," Kelly met my eyes and mouthed, "Yikes."

"What did I ask you to do?" Becky said.

"When?" Kelly looked confused.

"Earlier in your shift, I asked you to check on the copier issue in the back room," Becky said. "I just found out that Carrie went and fixed it instead."

"Oh, that. I was stuck on a long call. I honestly never use the copier and don't know much about it. Carrie is the expert on the copier. She was here when they installed it. So I asked if she could handle it. She was fine with it. Did she say something about it? She could have told me." Kelly had a great relationship with Carrie. They go bowling together on their off days. There is no way Carrie complained about Kelly, especially not to a new supervisor.

"Well, I asked you to do it, not Carrie." Becky pointed at Kelly.

I was personally appalled, and this wasn't happening to me.

"I'm sorry?" Kelly half-shrugged. I could tell she was also stunned. "I really would not have known how to fix it."

"Well, this is like the military, so when I tell you to do something, I am your commander, and you just do it."

I was floored.

Kelly didn't even speak. She just turned and walked back to her desk.

"Yeah, that's not at all true. This is not the military. We are absolutely allowed to question our supervisors. Especially if we feel they are not making the best decision. Kelly made the right call. Carrie was here when they installed the printer and was trained on how to fix it," I said. I didn't wait around for an answer.

A new priority one call needed to go out. I was steaming, though. I texted Kelly on my personal phone and told her that she should document the incident and send it to upper management immediately. I assured her that she did nothing wrong and that I had her back. She thanked me, and we moved on.

Or so I thought.

I had to stay over that morning on overtime in a call-taking role. It was a little past 7:00am at this point. I got a call from a woman who said she wanted an ambulance. I screened the call for medical issues, and she cited none.

"Ma'am, what do you need an ambulance for if you aren't hurt or sick?" I asked.

"Send me a goddamn ambulance so I can get home," she screamed.

"The ambulances don't give people rides to their homes. So if I sent you an ambulance and you wanted transport, they can only take you to a hospital. That's per their contract," I explained.

"Well, then send me the police. I don't mind riding in the back," she said.

"I can't do that either."

"Why not?" she asked.

"The police cannot give you a ride home. You need to take a taxi, Uber, Lyft, or even the bus." Providing alternative options isn't required of me, but she did sound possibly intoxicated. I was trying to give her the benefit of the doubt.

"I do not have the money for any of that," she screamed. "Send me the police right now and have them give me a ride home!"

"Ma'am, I have explained to you twice now that it is not an option." I was starting to get annoyed.

"Why is it, not an option? Get them here, right now, you stupid son of a bitch," she said, still screaming.

"Ok, there is no need for name-calling. The police cannot give rides. They have to be available for in-progress emergencies," I said, probably slightly elevated, but I wasn't yelling.

"What? So they can't give me a ride because they have to go to emergencies or whatever?" She asked.

"Yes, exactly." I think I was finally getting through to her. She called me some more horrible names and eventually hung up on me.

"God damn. What a piece of work," I said.

A red emergency message popped up on my screen: SEE ME IMMEDIATELY. It was from Becky at the supervisor's desk.

This ought to be good.

I walked to her desk and stood silently.

"Are you having a bad day?" Becky asked me.

"Why do you ask?" I know how these power plays go. I've dealt with many workplace bullies in my day.

"Well, first you snapped at me, and now you're screaming at callers," she said.

I was beside myself.

I really wanted to yell at her, but I like to think I've matured, so I collected myself for half a beat.

"I did not mean to snap at you, but Kelly did not deserve to be treated so poorly. First, you were incorrect in telling her this is a military-style command. She did nothing wrong by asking Carrie to look at the printer. Secondly, I did not scream at my caller. My caller was screaming at me. I had to be a little bit louder so she could hear me over her own screaming. I was quite calm dealing with her," I said.

"You do not tell me what to do around here. Do you understand?" Becky said firmly.

"You know what, if you have anything further to say to me, it needs to be in writing. This conversation is over. Thank you." I walked away.

I know how conversations like this end. It does not go well for the subordinate. I would rather she put it in writing that I was rude or disrespectful on my call. It is recorded, and she would have to prove that on her own.

The best thing at that moment was for me to walk away.

One of the dayshift guys shot me a sympathetic glance.

"Did you hear all that?" I asked him.

"Yeah," he said.

"Can I mark you down as a witness on this email I'm about to write?" I asked.

"Absolutely."

February 17TH, 2015 – 12 Hour Shift

I wish we could focus on the caller's drama and not have to deal with all the drama in the comm center," I said.

"Did something else happen with Becky?" Laura had not been the target of any Becky attacks, but she'd witnessed several on other dispatchers.

"I think when I stood up for Kelly, it put a target on my back. She is always hovering around me, waiting for me to slip up, even a little bit, to get me in trouble."

I did not feel comfortable at work when Becky was around. I was constantly questioning myself, ensuring my decision would align with the policy before making any. I know that sounds like something we should always strive to do, but we have over a thousand pages of policy, and it is impossible to reference every time we must make any decision.

"Has she done anything?"

"Nothing specific, but I also avoid her like the plague. I do not even recognize her existence. She will say hello, and I just walk by as if I heard nothing."

"By the way, what ever happened that morning? Did she write you up?" Laura asked.

"I get the impression that she tried. Audrey asked about the incident. I didn't include her in the email I sent to the higher-ups, so someone must have talked to her about it," I said.

"Oh? What did she say?" Laura asked.

"Not much, actually. She just wanted to hear from my perspective what happened. So I explained to her everything that transpired. She was shocked about the military comments and even thanked me for standing up for Kelly."

Audrey knows that I have a sharp tongue sometimes, but she also knows that my heart is always in the right place, I'm an excellent dispatcher, and she trusts my decisions.

"I told Audrey I wanted to say much more than I did, but I held back and tried to be respectful. She said she wants me to keep her in the loop of anything happening."

"Well, that's nice. At least you know Audrey has your back," Laura said.

Ultimately it wouldn't matter. Becky was determined to make all our lives miserable.

A new call came in.

The RP was trying to order a pizza. A story went viral on Facebook a while back about how if you're ever in a bad situation, you can call 911 and pretend to order a pizza, and the 911 dispatcher will understand that it's code for an emergency. It happens more often than you would think. The call-taker noted that it sounded more like a prank than someone under duress. They placed it as a priority two.

I agreed with their decision but decided to upgrade it to a priority one, just in case something more nefarious happened.

In the end, it was a couple of kids playing around. They got a reprimand from the officers and a reminder that 911 is not for prank calls.

I didn't think about it again.

About an hour later, Jon came to relieve me for my break.

"Dragon lady wants to see you at her desk on your way to break," Jon said.

"Oh god, did she say why?" I asked.

"Nope." He took over my desk. "Anything going on?"

"Negative," I said and headed toward the supervisor's desk.

"Good luck."

I approached the supervisor's desk in my usual fashion. Not saying a word, hands at my side, trying to stay as neutral as possible. She did not acknowledge me standing there, and I would not bite. I knew she saw me, so I waited another 45 seconds. Nothing, so I walked away to take my break.

"Excuse me," Becky called from behind me. I turned around and just stared. "You need to ask permission before you change the priority codes."

"Is that all?" I asked.

She did not answer.

I turned back and walked away. I was pissed. I didn't even eat my lunch. I grabbed my phone, pulled up the mobile site where we keep our 1000-page policy manual, and went to work. I located the policy on Type Code changes and emailed it to myself. I got back to my desk early and printed out a copy. I highlighted the part where the policy states that the priority codes may be changed if the dispatcher deems it necessary. The dispatcher needs to only document their justification of why it was upgraded or downgraded on the call.

I pulled up the call I was working on and printed it out. Then, I highlighted the portion of the call where I documented "Upgraded for possible exigent circumstances due to the caller not being able to speak freely." Then, I returned to the supervisor's desk with my papers in hand.

"I printed the policy for you from the manual, which it shows that I did, in fact, follow protocol to the letter. I also respectfully remind you that if you need to reprimand me for anything, I require it in writing as per our union contract," I said calmly. I avoided any tone that could be misconstrued as sarcasm.

I even impressed myself.

"Ok," was all Becky could mutter. She took the papers, and I returned to my desk to get my radio back from Jon.

"Fuck, now I'm hungry," I said.

"Didn't I just let you up to go eat?" Jon asked.

I fake laughed and explained to him what I did instead.

"You have too many convictions, but you're a young man. You'll grow out of it."

March 10ᵀᴴ, 2015 – 8 Hour Shift

Did you hear what happened last night?" Laura asked.

I spun around in my chair. "What?"

"With Mandy and Becky?" Laura said.

I shook my head.

"I guess they almost got into a fistfight on the floor."

"For real? What the hell?"

"I don't know all the details, but Mandy was working on something, and Becky came in early to relieve her. She was like almost thirty minutes early. Mandy had been working on this barricaded subject most of the morning and was finishing her supervisory tasks but needed a few more minutes."

Laura turned to look at her computer. "Copy Charlie 17 en route. Do you need a backing unit?"

After a second. "Copy."

Laura again gave me her attention, "Anyway, Mandy tells Becky that she's mostly done and needs a few more minutes. Becky starts getting pushy about her taking forever to finish the task and leave. Becky said that she came in early to let Mandy go early, and now she wasn't taking advantage of her generosity."

"What a psycho. I still can't see Mandy moving to violence, though," I said.

"Oh, she didn't. Mandy tells Becky she needs a few minutes to finish the task. She explained that although she was grateful for the early release, she was not expecting it and therefore had no way to plan for it."

Laura looked back to her screen.

I double check mine.

"So, Mandy finishes and walks out but realizes she left her purse at the desk. When she walks back in, she comes up from behind and hears Becky talking shit about Mandy to whoever was working on the desk next to her."

"Yikes," I said.

"Mandy confronts her about it politely. She asked to talk to Becky off the floor about it. Instead, Becky gets all confrontational right in front of everyone. Mandy says that the whole interaction is unprofessional and she'd rather discuss this off the floor in private. Apparently, Becky lunged towards Mandy."

"Holy shit! Did she throw a punch?" I asked, in genuine shock.

"I don't think so," Laura said. "I don't know much more than that."

"Well, that's quite a bit. Did she get suspended? Or in trouble at all?" I asked.

"No idea."

"Do any of us know Mandy well enough to reach out and see if she's ok?" I asked.

Generally, the shifts stick together. Graveyard workers and dayshift workers are natural-born enemies, and there is not a lot of social mixing. Graveyard shift resents dayshift for having the most effortless shift and never showing up on time to relieve us. Dayshift hates graveyard because they think they are lazy and complain about the pile-up of calls they have to deal with immediately in the morning.

"I don't have her number," Laura said.

"Me either."

The news of the night before was pretty much all anyone could talk about.[4] I heard a few more variations from other people. One guy told me that they threw a few punches. I reminded him that if that happened, Becky would be in jail.

Audrey was too much of a professional to discuss any actions of her colleagues. I honestly doubted she knew much. She keeps her nose in her own business; I've always respected that about her.

Terrance stopped by our desks, presumably on his way to break. "Want to hear something funny?"

"Only if it's not about Becky and Mandy's performance yesterday," I said.

"Ha. No. I had a call from the Arby's, and this man said this guy is clowning in the parking lot. So I asked him what is he doing? He explains that he's walking around the parking lot rubbing up on people, groping them. The guy is super drunk."

"This isn't starting out very funny, Terrance," Laura said, raising an eyebrow.

I had confidence in him.

"Just wait. I get the description. He said it was a black male, 20s, 5 foot 7, heavier build with white and red face paint,

---

[4] When the 911 lines aren't providing us with our daily dose of drama, we have plenty from within the comm center.

clown costume, and giant oversized shoes. I was like, so when you said he was clowning, you meant literally a clown? And he said yes. So, now we have a call about a drunk clown molesting people in an Arby's parking lot," Terrance laughed.

"I have had almost that exact nightmare," I said.

I wish I was exaggerating these stories to make this book more interesting. But I assure you, I am not.

March 20TH, 2015 – 12 Hour Shift

A man called 911 to tell me he had a parrot stuck in his car," Jon said.

Jon was here to give Laura a break.

"A parrot?" I asked.

"Yeah, he was at the grocery store, letting the parrot free roam in the car. He left the car keys in the vehicle by mistake but wasn't worried because he didn't lock it. The parrot stepped on the lock button, and now the parrot is trapped in the car," Jon said.

"That's a new one. Did you tell him to call a locksmith?" I know Jon knows what to do, but I don't know what else to ask.

"He already called one, but the weather delayed them. It's nasty out there tonight. Did you see how much snow we are getting?" Jon asked. "I ended up putting in a call."

"Wow, really? For a bird?" I was shocked. "I can't see you taking pity on a bird."

"It's a parrot," Jon corrected. "His name is Petey, and he's thirty years old. That parrot was his life, and with the delay from the locksmith, the parrot could have died. I checked the screen first and saw that the city units weren't super busy."

"I mean, we would do it for a dog."

I was still shocked by Jon's generosity tonight. I've known the man for a couple years, and I'm still learning.

"Oh my fucking god, look at the jail roster right now," Kelly interrupted.

"Ok, what am I looking for?" I pulled it up and started scanning.

"No, just look at the most recent booked," she said.

I scanned for any familiar names and, "What the hell?" I gasped. "No way. That has to be someone with the same name? No freaking way!"

"Way. I looked it up on Twitter, and it is her," she said.

"Who?" Jon asked.

"Becky is the newest resident of our county jail," Kelly said. I looked at the charges. Assault 4th Degree with DV notated. Coworkers would not be considered domestic violence. We spend enough time together. It feels like it should. But legally speaking, no, coworkers are not domestic violence partners. Even if Mandy pressed charges, she wouldn't be arrested for assault if she didn't throw a punch. Either way, it wouldn't be for domestic violence.

"What happened?" I asked.

"Only rumors at this point, but apparently, she got into a fistfight with her partner and knocked her unconscious," Laura said.

"Does she live in town?" I asked, curious if our guys arrested her. There would be a report we could look up. It wouldn't be the most professional move, but we could.

"Of course not. She lives just on the outskirts of our jurisdiction," Laura said.

Great minds and all.

"Damn," I felt a bit of schadenfreude. "I hope that's the last we have to deal with Becky."

It was not.

13

Don't Read This If You Can't Handle The B Word

Dispatch: 911, Where is your emergency?
Male Caller: My wife is pregnant, and she is having contractions.
Dispatch: Ok, how far along is she?
Male Caller: I don't know. She's due October 11!
Dispatch: What pregnancy is this for her?
Male Caller: What?
Dispatch: Does she have other children?
Male Caller: Oh, yes. She has three kids.
Dispatch: So, this will be her fourth kid. How far along are the contractions?
Male Caller: I don't know.
Dispatch: Ok, have you been timing them?
Male Caller: No!
Dispatch: Alright, we can time them together. Let me know when she starts her next one, ok?
Male Caller: How in the hell am I supposed to know?
Dispatch: Just have her tell you when the next one starts. Are you right next to her?
Male Caller: No, she's being a bitch in the next room.
Dispatch: Uhhmm, can you go be next to her so we can help her?
Male Caller: Ugh, fine! They want to know shit from you. *throws the phone at his pregnant wife*
Dispatch: Hello?
Female Caller: Hello?
Dispatch: Hi, this is 911. Are you ok?
Female Caller: Yeah, I just need to get to the hospital soon. These contractions are getting close together.
Dispatch: How far apart are they now?
Female Caller: About 3-4 minutes apart.

Dispatch: Do you have a clean blanket or some towels nearby?

Female Caller: No. *struggling in obvious pain*

Dispatch: Ok, can I speak to your husband again?

Male Caller: What? *In an outraged voice*

Dispatch: I need you to find a blanket and some clean towels.

Male Caller: For what? Aren't you sending an ambulance?

Dispatch: Yes, but her contractions are really close together, and we need to be ready in case the baby comes before the ambulance arrives. Can you see if any part of the baby is visible?

Male Caller: I don't have time for this shit.

Dispatch: Can you please just—

Male Caller: She's being a bitch, and I've got other shit I need to do.

Dispatch: I don't know why you are so upset. Can you please just check to see if she's delivering?

Male Caller: *to his wife* They want to know if you're delivering now.

Female Caller: *mumbles in the background*

Male Caller: *yelling and cursing at his wife incoherently*

Female Caller: FUCK YOU!

Dispatch: Ok, it sounds like the ambulance may be there… can you please unlock the door?

They sound like wonderful people," Laura said, hanging up the phone. "That poor woman."

"I hope you sent the police on that one too. That sounded like a whole mess of a domestic situation," Terrance said.

"Oh yeah. I even gave the responding medic crew a heads up on the ongoing drama."

"I had an eerily similar one once. Except the husband didn't call, he just bailed. Apparently, he was upset that she was too busy going into labor to take care of dinner. So I spoke with the older son, fifteen years old?" I said.

"What is with all of these trash men?" Laura asked.

Terrance was offended. "Must be what you women are attracted to because nice guys like me sit here single and childless while women have several babies with these trash men,' and apparently misguided."

"Uh, I don't think that is quite right. 'Nice guys' assume that they are the ultimate specimen of men and gaslight women into these situations where they think they are making a good decision with a nice guy, but it turns out that they are, in fact, the very trash of which we're talking," I said.

"Are you saying that I am a trash man?" Terrance asked.

"Not necessarily, but saying that you're this nice guy who does not get the women he wants makes you sound like you're trying to invoke guilty emotions out of women," I said. "It's about control. You said assholes get all the women, and nice guys get left out. That kind of behavior is what someone trying to control another's emotions would say. I'm not saying this is your intention, but it's how you're coming off. I'd say, change your approach."

"Really?" Terrance asked.

I could tell I caught him off guard. I've known the guy for a while. I think there's probably a girl out there for him, but he needs to grow in confidence first.

"You are a great guy, Terrance, but Jackson is correct. I think all these trash men start out as the *nice guy* and, through coercion and gaslighting, end up exposing themselves for the assholes they are. Most of these women are victims," Laura said.

Time for a change of subject.

Laura agreed. "So, what happened with your call?" she asked.

"Oh! Right, so the fifteen-year-old son was such a sweetheart to his mom. He got all the towels for her and even delivered his baby brother right there on the phone with me. I got to hear the baby crying over the phone. It was so sweet," I said

"Awww, that's awesome. I still haven't had a full delivery on the phone yet," Terrance said.

"It was even cooler than that," I said. "After we delivered the baby, I got more of the story. The father left because he didn't believe that she was in labor. She didn't even know she was pregnant."

"Wait, what?" Laura asked.

"She said she was pregnant but had a miscarriage about a month into it. She said she kept getting spotty periods every month and didn't gain any weight. However, that night, she said she started feeling labor pains. She said she know what labor was. She's got two kids, and this is labor. I took over with her son from there." It really was an extraordinary story.

"I bet they named him after you," Terrance joked.

"Haha. Let's hope not."

February 18TH, 2019 – 12 Hour Shift

Jackson, please stop referring to yourself as a master baker," Audrey said with feigned annoyance.

"I thought you tried one of my scones?" I asked.

"I did, and I agree that they cannot be beaten. However, calling yourself a master baker in the workplace feels inappropriate."

"I can teach you how to make scones if it's a jealousy concern," I said.

"It is not a jealousy concern, and you know it."

"Audrey, we can master-bake together. I can teach you."

"Stop!" Audrey laughed and walked away.

"We can do it back-to-back if you feel more comfortable, but it will be hard for me to show you how to do it!"

Is there anything I could say that would be more inappropriate than what the callers say to us?

No, probably not.

I have been called every name in the book. Sometimes entirely out of the blue. I've gone through an entire call with someone completely stable and congenial, and then at the end, I start closing up the call, and bam.

"I've put in a call for you, just watch for the officers, and we'll see you soon. Thanks."

"Fuck you, faggot." Then the disconnect.

It came completely out of nowhere.

The first time it happened, I was taken aback. I replayed the call for hints of anything I may have said wrong. Traces of the RP being upset by something I said.

Nothing.

Now when it happens, I think, *eh, all in a day*, and I move on. It does take years of being beaten down to get to this point, though.

Would not recommend it.

"Ma'am, please stop yelling. I can't understand you when you yell." Melanie was working with a problematic caller. She had all the signs, sitting straight in her chair, talking with her hands even though the caller couldn't see them, and a deep stare gaze on her face while talking. "Ma'am, I understand he is having a heart attack. Yes. Yes. I have," Melanie's voice hitched. "Ma'am, listen. Stop! I have a call started, and I have units en route, but I need to ask you a few more questions so we can try to help your father."

"People need to chill and let us help them," Terrance said. We were both eavesdropping on Melanie's struggle.

"I just got called a cunt," Melanie said.

"Oh no, this can't be the first time?" I asked before I saw the instant confusion on her face. "No, I don't mean it like that. I get called all sorts of names on the 911 lines. This cannot be your first time being called a mean name by a caller."

"No, I just don't know when I'll get used to it."

"A few more years," I said. "Or we all just turn into Jon."

"A fate worse than death," Melanie said.

"What are you two staring at?" Jon asked, walking by our stations.

"Nooooooooooooooooothing," we sang in unison.

"Did you hear about his dog call the other day?" I asked.

"Dog call?" Melanie asked.

259

I spun around in my chair to pull up my archives folder and looked for the file I saved on Jon's dog call.

"Come listen to this bad boy," I said, opening the file. I adjusted the speakers to be loud enough for us but not loud enough to disturb the room.

"911, what is the address of your emergency?" Jon asked.

"I'm on Highway 1 at mile marker six, and I *inaudible*," said a distraught female who was crying through her words.

"Ok, highway 1 milepost 6. What are you reporting?"

*Inaudible mumble-crying. *

"Take a deep breath for a second and repeat. I can't understand you," Jon said calmly.

Inaudible mumbling again

"Again, ma'am, I can't understand anything you're saying. Clearly, you're upset, but I need you to try to calm down just a bit so I can understand what you need." Jon was calm, deliberate, and professional.

"I just hit a… *inaudible*," the crying continued.

"You were in a vehicle collision?" Jon asked?

"Yeah," she cried even harder.

"Ok, is the other driver still there?"

"Noooo," the sobbing continued.

"Which way did the other driver go? Northbound or Southbound?" Jon asked.

"Noo," she sobbed.

"What do you mean? I'm trying to figure out where the guy that hit you went so we can maybe catch him," Jon explained.[1]

---

[1] Sometimes the reminder of punishment for another person who wronged

"No other car. I hit—hit—a—" the crying continued.

"I'm sorry, you hit what?" he asked. The crying continued, and we could not understand what this woman was trying to say. "What did you hit?"

"A DOG!" she screamed.

"Oh, ok. This is a vehicle versus dog collision. Alright, so is the owner nearby?" Jon asked.

The crying was too much. I love animals, too, and would be devastated if I hit a dog. But I've had calls where people hit children, and they weren't this intense.

"Hello? Ma'am, can you please try and focus for just another minute. I need a few more things, and we can get off the phone. Is this owner there with you?"

"NO! I DON'T KNOW WHOSE DOG THIS IS!" she screamed.

The poor lady shouldn't have done that.

"Ok, can you separate yourself from the dog so I can get your name and number?" Jon asked. The struggle continued for another forty-five seconds, trying to get basic information. "Ok, we will get someone out there as soon as possible."

"Wait," she said.

"What?" I could hear the disdain in Jon's voice.

"Am I going to get in trouble for this?" she asked.

"What?"

"Will I get in trouble for hitting this dog?" she asked. Her voice was as clear as day as if she wasn't whaling on the phone for the last five minutes.

---

them will focus their attention.

"I don't know. I haven't gotten the dog's side of the story yet," Jon said and hung up on her.

I looked over at Melanie; she was a mixture of amusement and shock. I closed the program and looked around for Jon. But, unfortunately, he wasn't in earshot.

"Did he get in trouble for that?" Melanie asked.

"Of course not."

August 3RD, 2017 – 12 Hour Shift

I got a call from a nurse reporting her patient was non-verbal, brain-dead, and all he could do was blink. At first, I thought oh, that's sad. Then, I compared it to working here. Eh, I'd take it." Jon said.

"We all wish you were non-verbal, Jon," Carrie said.

The quiet slayer.

At my communication center, about one-third of our calls are medical or fire-related, and two-thirds are a mix of police calls and nonsense. When people call 911 for non-emergency reasons, we try suggesting alternate solutions for their problems. Unfortunately, more often than not, they don't want to hear it. They want to have all of their problems solved by others.

By us.

I hung up with a woman who had a cat stuck up in a tree. Our firefighters will not respond to this kind of call. Therefore, it falls in our lap as dispatchers. Most of us have go-to solutions.

Carrie tells people to leave some food at the base of the tree, and after a little while, the cat will come down on its own. I tend to remind people that the cat got itself up there and will be able to get down on its own. Jon will ask the caller, "Have you ever seen a cat skeleton in a tree?"

"Ma'am, please let me send you an ambulance?" Carrie said, louder than her usual tone. "Ok, well, please call us back if you change your mind."

"What was that all about?" Jon asked.

"This woman was having an issue with her husband's oxygen machine and couldn't get ahold of the company."

"Probably because it's almost five in the morning," Jon said.

"Exactly. I explained that to her and offered her an ambulance. She was having none of it. She said that he had a backup tank that was functioning properly. She wanted me to try to call this company and make them come fix it."

"Did she think we have some secret after-hours number for the random company she uses hidden somewhere?" Jon asked.

"I guess. When I told her that all I could do was send out an ambulance crew, she interrupted me and told me not to bother them," Carrie chuckled to herself, "She didn't mind bothering me. I told her I wasn't calling this company on her behalf. She called me a miserable bitch, and then we moved on."

"Well, at least she got your name right," Jon said.

Carrie really has worked with him too long. She doesn't even flinch.

"Is it a full moon? People are really on something tonight," I said. "I also just got called a bitch."

"Wow, why are you a bitch?" Carrie asked.

"It started out with, *this isn't an emergency but* which, of course, is always my favorite on a 911 line. She wanted me to have an officer come out and arrest her friend as a prank."

"I can honestly say that's new for me," Carrie said.

"Yeah, and when I said that we can't do that, she asked why not. I told her I wasn't going to explain why sending an officer out to fake arrest someone and that she was now tying up a 911 line for people with real emergencies. She called me a little bitch and hung up."

"You should have sent an officer and real-arrested her for false reporting on a 911 line," Jon suggested.

"I wish that's how that worked," I laughed.

People ask us to do all sorts of weird things. I've been asked to call someone's boss, as the police, and tell them that they were sick.[2]

I did not.

Another guy wanted me to call a grocery store and ask them to lift his lifetime ban. I struggle to understand what they want me to do most of the time.

"There's a train blocking the roadway," an RP said. I looked at his GPS location on the phone.

"Oh, is this at 4th and Main Street?" I asked.

"Yeah," the RP replied.

"Yes, the train, unfortunately, hit a car," I said, ready for the conversation to be over.

---

[2] The invention of Vine followed by TikTok made this worse for a while.

"Yes, I saw that, but the train is blocking the roadway," the RP said.

"Right," I am failing to connect with this caller. "The train hit a car and is now unable to move."

"Yes. It's blocking the road."

"Right. It's probably going to be blocking it for a while. What are you trying to report?"

Maybe I'm missing something?

"The road is BLOCKED, YOU IDIOT!"

Sincerely, I did not understand what he wanted me to do about it. I tried to explain to him that the train would not be able to move for quite a while. He should try to follow the instructions of the on-site crew and find an alternate way around the incident. He continued to yell at me about the train in the roadway. I got nowhere with him and ended the call.

I think that's one of the misconceptions people have about 911 dispatchers, that we must remain on the phone with them.

Untrue.

If I get what I need, the caller is uncooperative or rude, I am not required to stay on the line. Obviously, there are exceptions. For example, suppose the caller is mentally unstable and inappropriate but is actively experiencing an in-progress, life-threatening emergency. In that case, I will endure the abuse and stay with them until the police arrive. On the other hand, if they don't have a true emergency and just want to yell and degrade me, I've got better things to do.

December 13TH, 2018 – 8 Hour Shift

Are you trying to do a sting operation to trap your drug dealer?" Terrance asked, and all of our heads perked up. "Uhm, I guess I can send an officer out to talk to you about that. Can I get your name?"

"What the hell was that about?" I asked after Terrance hung up with his caller.

"Apparently, she was upset with the quality of her recent meth delivery and wants to turn her dealer in," Terrance said.

"That seems kind of dangerous," but what do I know.

"Yeah, isn't the mantra snitches get stitches?" Terrance said.

"One would assume."

The public would be shocked if they knew how many random bodies, or body parts, we find in a year. I am not saying they are all drug-related, but some must be.

We have a few homeless encampments around town. Occasionally, the health department will sweep these camps, and we regularly find bodies. Once, we found a female's body in the middle of a trash pile at the edge of an encampment. She was missing her head. Not a single media outlet picked up the story. An investigation was started into a homicide, but I'm sure it's still unresolved. I remember looking it up about a year later, and the woman was a known drug abuser, homeless, and had no next-of-kin to even contact. Fingerprints returned no results for a missing person report.

She was deceased, nobody cared, and we never found the head.

"We found a hand once inside of a pressure cooker that was duct-taped under a pier," Carrie said.

"A human hand?" I asked, already knowing the answer.

"Yes. It was a problem for us because when a pressure cooker duct-taped to the bottom of a pier was found, we assumed it was an explosive."

"Oh shit."

"Yeah, we had to call out the dive team and the bomb squad. We had a neighboring agency assist us too. We had to clear out the entire area by a half-a-mile radius for several hours," Carrie said, "Finally, they somehow determined that it wasn't an explosive and opened it up to find a human hand."

"Did they ever figure out who it belonged to?"

"Nope." That's it.

That's all we ever got. We found a hand under a pier, inside a pressure cooker. I could have invented an ending for this for you, but I want you to know how I feel on a near-daily basis.

It is probably unfair to assume that these found body parts are all drug-related crimes. No other solutions come to mind, and maybe this is my way of solving it in my head to make it make sense. It comforts me that, since I don't get involved with the drugs and crime on the streets, my hand probably won't end up in a pressure cooker taped under a pier one day.

It's easy to make up stories and answers for the weird things around town, but the truth is often stranger than fiction.

An RP called to report she was a dumpster diver, and while she was out diving through a complex's dumpster, she located a box with a human head inside of it.

I know immediately what you're thinking, we've found the head of the woman from the encampment.

You would be wrong.

Apparently, the RP misspoke. She did not find a head but rather a skull. A preserved skull. One that you could purchase for science purposes. It was not clear if it was even real. According to the officer, it looked real enough, and we put it in evidence just to cover our bases. The officer said they did due diligence and asked around the apartment complex if anyone knew anything about the skull. No one admitted to anything. Another unsolved strange occurrence for the list.

"I can't handle people today," Laura said, sitting beside me.

"It's a good thing you didn't pick a profession where you have to handle people," I added.

"This woman honestly had a legitimate call, but she also had a lot of trouble staying focused on the information I needed to get," Laura sighed and logged in to her dispatch terminal. "I could not control the conversation well enough, and she kept spouting all this unrelated information."

"What was the complaint?"

"She found a foot."

I shook my head in disbelief.

"Yeah, she told me that she woke up at exactly 6:45 am and got out the door to take her dog for a walk, which she always does by 7:00 am, or the dog will pee on the floor. She thought about going down her usual route through Perkin's Park but decided today, for unknown reasons, to head down to the beach. Blah, blah, blah."

I just laughed because I know this type of caller all too well. Too many details and not enough immediately pertinent information.

"I interrupted and asked what she was trying to report, and she got all offended and said, I'm *trying* to tell you. She gets sassy with me, so I let her ramble on about forgetting breakfast before finally telling me she gets to the beach and finds a foot. It was in a shoe, on the beach. I asked if there were any other body parts. She gets indignant and says, if there were other body parts, don't you think I would have told you already?"

"Wow, she really got under your skin," I said. I rarely see Laura this worked up.

"I am trying to assist this woman, but she's not letting me. So I finally got a call started. Officers get on the scene, and it's just a shoe with some gunk inside. It looked like a bone sticking out, but it was just a weirdly shaped rock. The officer messaged me on CAD and told me she said that her 911 dispatcher was a complete bitch."

We both laughed at that.

"I always wondered if some of these difficult callers complain to the officers about us," I said.

Apparently, they sometimes do. Of course, we get complaints about the officers all the time, so it's par for the course, I guess.

All complaints get investigated for both officers and the dispatchers, depending on the nature of the complaint. I've had a few complaints get investigated. Most of which were unfounded. People are just upset with the outcome and not really with me. I was professional. They were just upset with the things I had to tell them.

In my tenure, I've had one founded complaint, and I admit to it. I was rude to the caller and did not have to be. They got under my skin, and I yelled a bit at them. I don't even remember what was said. It was unprofessional, I got talked about it, and we moved on.[3]

In this world, I like to believe you get what you give. Even if you're a bitch, we will still assist you if you are in your hour of need. It's what we get paid to do. It's what we love to do. Saving people is our calling. Please try to understand that our questions are not there to annoy you or piss you off.

Just be kind. We will strive to do the same.

---

[3] You know I would tell you if I could remember. I think it was their tone more than their words that really cut me. I matched their energy.

14
Technology: It Is Not Like TV Or The Movies

Dispatch: 911, Where is your emergency?
Female Caller: I don't know.
Dispatch: Ok, what is the address of the emergency?
Female Caller: I don't know where I am.
Dispatch: Ok, do you know what city you are in?
Female Caller: No.
Dispatch: Ok, well, I can't send help if I don't know where you are.
Female Caller: I am outside. I'm waiving at the satellites. Can't you just use the computer thing and see me?

I wish I could tell you I was making up the transcript above for a good story. However, that is an actual 911 call. Part of the reason I wanted to write this book is because of all of the misinformation that is out there about our abilities. Misinformation perpetuated in movies, TV, and even the news makes our job more difficult.

Many callers get upset that we do not know their exact location the second that they call 911. As a result, they often refer to our GPS systems.

Sometimes, I can understand the frustration. I think it is unfortunate that you can hail an Uber or even get a pizza delivered to yourself based on your GPS system but not an ambulance. I wish we could see the phone's GPS location when someone calls in. But 911 isn't an app for your phone.

Yet.

I've heard rumors that upgrades are being worked on, but I have not seen anything in the works. It was also rumored that we cannot see you via your GPS information because of privacy concerns. Maybe we could design a system where the user could opt out of sharing their GPS data if they have a concern?

I don't know.

I don't make the decisions. I promise.

We've reviewed the phone tracing details for 911 in chapter one. We get a rough idea based on the phase of the ping from the last used tower. Sometimes, it is accurate, but when your life is on the line, I would much rather you tell me exactly where you are rather than rely on technology that has failed us before.

December 12TH, 2016 – 12 Hour Shift

As a 911 dispatcher, I have access to some excellent tools to assist me in my job. However, not all 911 centers are created equally, and I only speak directly to my own experiences in this part. In addition, communication centers in different states might have access to other systems or no systems.

In my state, in my center, we are allowed to ping a cell phone for its geographical location if the situation is deemed exigent.

What does this mean?

If a 911 dispatcher deems it necessary. This looks like the number has dialed 911, and based on what is heard, there is reason to suspect an immediate threat to someone's life. At that point, the lawful ability presents itself to ping a phone. As you can imagine, there are a lot of laws surrounding when and how I can do this.

It is not legal to ping a cell phone to find someone who has run away of their own volition. No matter how concerned the family member may be. I can't ping a cell phone just because the person has a warrant out for their arrest, which drives some officers crazy. I am not allowed to ping a cheating girlfriend's phone to find out where she was on Friday night when she said she was at her mother's, even if someone knows her mother is on a work trip.[1]

I have to believe and prove that an immediate threat to life exists. It is difficult, and we end up pinging phones much less than you would think.

"Jackson, can you look at this call?" Melanie just graduated from radio school, and I told her I'd look over any call for her whenever needed.

"Always," I said, "What's the number?"

"672."

It was a strange one indeed. It was a request for assistance from a neighboring agency. They wanted assistance with a missing person's case from a different jurisdiction.

"Uh, wow. Why do they think this guy is in our jurisdiction?" I asked.

"It says near the bottom that they believe he camps in our county, somewhere along the water," Melanie said.

I don't know how I missed that.

---

[1] In Aspen, for a week, because I helped her with her PowerPoint presentation.

"That could be so many places. I don't even know where to start with this one."

"Yeah. That doesn't make it easy. Did you try running his license plate to see if we have ever had contact with him?" While I am pulling at strings here, sometimes thinking outside of the box is most helpful.

"No. I'll try that," Melanie said and turned back around.

A challenge.

Excitement wells up inside of me. I love solving puzzles, but I needed more information. So, I called the original agency, who reported him as missing. They told me his mother reported him as missing in their hometown. He went camping alone on the coast, and she thought it was most likely in our neighboring jurisdiction. The man was overdue to return and did not check in at work. It was very unlike him. He loved his job and had not expressed any suicidal ideation.

"No contacts with this vehicle at all," Melanie said as I hung up the phone.

"I need to call the 2nd dispatch center now and try to find out why they think he's in our jurisdiction," I said.

I spoke with a nice call-taker who wasn't familiar with the case, but she put me on hold to find the person who had called us initially.

While on hold, I listened to Melanie talk to Mike The Dick about the call.

"We're not allowed to ping a cell phone for a missing person. We have no way of knowing whether this person meant to disappear. It's their right to privacy," Mike The Dick explained.

He was, in fact, a dick, and I stand by that.

However, he was not wrong.

I spoke with the other PSAP supervisor, who explained that they felt this disappearance was exigent and they already pinged his cell phone. It showed him located in our jurisdiction, along the coast. Unfortunately, she couldn't say precisely where, and I couldn't see the ping map because they use a different CAD system than us. He noted that it was Verizon Wireless, and I could ping the cell phone myself. I didn't want to explain to him that we could not do that, so I simply said thank you and disconnected.

"Well, we are in somewhat of a pickle," I said.

"What now?" Melanie asked.

"Their supervisor said that they pinged the phone."

Melanie's face scrunched up.

"I know, they really shouldn't have, but whatever. That's not our problem. Our problem is, they basically heard it's not your jurisdiction and then stopped listening, so we don't know exactly where it was pinging."

"Can't they just send us over the CFS?" Melanie was thinking critically, and I loved it.

"Nope. That's the east PSAP. This one uses a completely different system. If I call Verizon, I wonder if they'd release the information to me based on their ping and not request a new one from us?"

I considered running this plan through Mike The Dick but decided it would be better to beg for forgiveness than ask for permission.

Verizon answered, and I explained the situation. They called the 911 center and verified my employment with one of my colleagues. I explained thoroughly that I was not requesting a new ping. I was simply seeking the legacy records of the ping they did for our neighboring agency. Thankfully, they were understanding and gave me the GPS coordinates. I plugged it into google maps, and we had a starting place.

"Thank you so much for your assistance on this," Melanie said. She dispatched the call to a unit.

"Not a problem at all. You see how dynamic this can be. Sometimes, we must dig in and do what we can to figure out these problems. It's actually one of my favorite parts of this job."[2]

They found the missing camper after all. It got cold at night, and he used a camping stove for heat, but there was no proper ventilation, and he died. He poisoned himself in his sleep. Hopefully, a peaceful end for him and some closure for his mother, who had been worried all weekend about her son.

September 9TH, 2014 – 12 Hour Shift

Another great tool in my arsenal is a program that accesses driving and vehicle records in my entire state. Immediately, this does not sound impressive. Most folks would expect we could run an individual by name and a vehicle by its plate or VIN number.

True.

---

[2] Makes me feel like a fancy CSI.

However, I can use this tool and run vehicles and people by specific algorithms and get hits based on very little information.

For example, if an RP tells me, she sees a child abducted by a white man in his 40s with a full grey beard. He was approximately five foot seven, 190 pounds, with brown hair and driving a large white Chevy Van, and she did not get a license plate. Not a whole lot to go off, right? I can punch in what I know to this system and get a return on all vehicles in the state that match.

I can narrow it down by probability and area. I can have the RP estimate the approximate vehicle year and narrow it even further. I can take a list of 1000 vehicles and keep trimming it down until I have a more manageable list. But, again, it is not an exact science, and if the vehicle is not registered in my state, I will not be able to find it.[3]

It's simply a tool.

"City units, report of a shooting, 14th and Arbor. The suspects were inside a newer black Dodge Charger that was last seen heading eastbound on 14th. The possible weapon was a handgun. The caller did not see the plates. One possible victim shot in the leg," Laura said.

My ears perked up at her broadcast.

"Jealous. The most exciting call I have right now is a neighbor dispute over some lawn decorations," I said.

"Well, you could broadcast it as info since the car was technically headed to your area," Laura said.

"Ok." I broadcasted what we knew.

---

[3] With this specific tool. Don't test me, I can find anyone.

"Apparently, it is the same vehicle as last week's shooting. Can you try to find that call for me? See if we had a plate on it that time?" Laura asked.

"On it!" I dug through the history page to find a shooting with a Dodge Charger from last week.

Success.

Kind of.

I located the call. "Yeah, it's 6745, but it doesn't have a plate either."

"Bummer," Laura said.

"Maybe I'll try digging through the vehicle website and see what I can find," I said.

Starting with reviewing the previous call for any details missed. The RP believed the vehicle was brand new. Additionally, I verified it was black. They said the driver was a white male in his mid-thirties, wearing a white and blue striped shirt and dark hair. I decided to start with the make and model. I searched for all brand-new black Dodge Chargers sold in my area within the last few months. I got a list of about 20. Not too bad. I narrowed it down to male owners in their thirties. The list was still about 17. I giggled at that.

"Well, I've got it down to 17 so far."

"Not too bad," Laura said.

"Any new information that may help narrow this down a bit?" I asked.

"Not yet."

The units got to the scene of the shooting.

The RP of last week's call was an uninjured passerby. No one was shot, therefore no victims to interview.

"Ok, they said the victim knows the guy who shot him. He goes by the name Big Jim. Maybe it would be registered to a James?" Laura said.

"I'll see what I can do."

Narrowing the search to add James or Jim to the registered owner resulted in two options. One James and one Jim. I ran both subjects through the computer. James had nothing on his record. Jim had been arrested for assault in a bar fight a few years ago. My money was on Jim. I added both profiles to the call just to be on the safe side.

"Sounds like you found Jim," Laura said, reviewing my updated notes. "Oh wait, which one is it?"

"If I were a betting man and there was a line on this in Vegas, I'd bet it all on the Jim who was arrested for the barfight. But I work in a dispatch center where I know about the stranger things, so I included both subjects to cover my bases."

"Ha. Well, we shall see."

Laura gave the units the information I located and sent a unit to each house. Success, it was Jim. They did not find the car that night but spoke with a family member who ratted him out. They were tired of the trauma that he was putting the family through.

I would like to think he was eventually arrested, arraigned, tried, and sentenced for his crimes, but as you already know, I have no idea.

Let's just say he was, so we can both sleep tonight.

April 30TH, 2017 – 12 Hour Shift

We keep logs of everything at the dispatch center. The more information we have on file, the better chances we have to help in situations where little information is provided.

A call from a cell phone came in on the 911 line. There was an audible struggle in the background. No one was responding to my questions, but there was shuffling, a female screaming, and a man yelling aggressively at her. The shuffling continued for another minute or so until the line went dead. This all happened within ten seconds. Her phone only pinged with Phase 1. There was little information to go off.

When I called the number back, it went to voicemail. Potentially, I heard something wrong. At this point, I probably have exigent circumstances to ping the phone and get a GPS location. It is quite a process that takes time, As I pointed out before, I need to prove beyond a reasonable doubt that someone's life is at stake. I can often get what I need from our archival records.

My first step at this point is to research the phone number. I look at the logs, which have every number that has ever called 911 in the past. If the phone number is incorrect, I'll check the registration, which is essentially our local phone book. This is, honestly, only a little bit more sophisticated than the book you get at your front door. It stores prior addresses and phone numbers for individuals.

For this case, I saw that the same number called 911 a year ago. At that point, the RP was a female named Sheila Brown, reporting a noisy neighbor. She lived at 1011 Main Street. I can cross-reference that location with the general ping from the Phase 1 phone call I just received. A decent enough match. It could have been pinging off the same tower as the downtown area.

Now, I have somewhere to start.

After creating the CFS, I looked to see who the dispatcher was.

It was Jon.

I let Jon know that I was still working on more information. Jon got a city unit to start towards Main Street to do a welfare check, but my work is not over yet.

Maybe Sheila got rid of her cell phone, and now someone else owns that number? I still get calls for Steve, who owned my personal cell number, and I have had this phone for over ten years.

Another option is that Sheila still has her cell phone, but maybe she moved. People move all the time. I run Sheila Brown through the Department of Licensing records and found a new address, 1405 Uptown Road. Based on the Phase 1 ping, that address could also make sense.

Sheila could be in either location at this point. Maybe she was at her sister's house on Main Street when she called in the noisy neighbor. I still do not have enough information. I am making educated guesses based on inexact details, hoping it will help.

At this point, I update Jon so he can tell the officer about the Department of Licensing address. The officer will first check the Main Street address because that is where we last spoke with the owner of the cell phone. Then, if that place is clear, the officer will check the Uptown Road location.

It does not stop there, though. I heard a second voice. Who was the man she was with yelling aggressively?

Now, I do a reverse search based on both addresses and see if I can find any history of a male at either place. Are any men registered with the Department of Licensing living at either place? I checked both and only found a man at the Uptown location. He called 911 to report a suspicious vehicle in the area about four years ago. My best guess, he was likely a previous tenant.

The ping process on the phone was still not started. We have some information to go off, albeit only slightly. I have a name and possible addresses. It is still faster to check both addresses and then go from there than to start the pinging process. Keeping in mind, of course, I would have to jump through legal hoops to ping. Whereas, at this point, I am just checking on the welfare of a citizen. It is also noteworthy that my other duties do not stop while all of this is happening. I am still taking other 911 calls. I still have radio transmissions to answer. Other officers are doing traffic stops and handling other calls.

911 dispatchers are masters of multitasking.[4]

The officer was able to locate Sheila Brown at the Uptown location. She was having a domestic dispute with her boyfriend. Thankfully it was verbal only, and he already left home. Sheila stated that she did not realize 911 had been called. Her phone was in her pocket.

No crime and no life was at stake.

---

[4] And I am the master of the masters. You should hear me roar!

Would I still have been able to prove exigent circumstances?

Maybe.

If the search at both locations proved unsuccessful, I would have attempted the ping when I was out of ideas based on my logs, history, and Department of Licensing addresses.

I do what I can to help on every single call.

Yes, it is exhausting.

December 11TH, 2015 – 12 Hour Shift

We do not speak in ten codes or any other sort of secret code at *my* center. Those are the rules my state follows.

A question that repeatedly gets asked about are secret codes.

"What's the code for a murder?" my uncle asked at dinner.

"What's the code for a bathroom break? And is there a different code if it's pee and poop? Like a 10-001 is a pee and a 10-002 is a poop?" a friend asked at cocktail hour.

"Do you have a code for a possible DUI so they don't know they've been caught?" my alcoholic grandma asked. Likely for research purposes.

I think this stems from past practices and the existence of 10 codes. 10 codes did exist, and I have heard that in many places, specific 10 codes still exist. Television and movies perpetuate this lie.

The problem we touched on earlier is that codes do not align with other agencies. For the most part, agencies speak plain English, and if you have a scanner or any of the online apps that can pick up police scanners, you'll know we abbreviate a lot. I firmly believe native English speakers should be able to understand what we are saying.

Brevity is huge in our industry. We need to acquire information promptly. Anything could go south. Transmissions over 30 seconds should be broken up so that a responder in the field can interrupt and get help if needed. To shorten our transmissions, we speak a particular cadence so we can convey mass amounts of information quickly. If you haven't noticed, reports from citizens can get quite lengthy.

"My name is Marilyn Johnson, I live at 1234 Orange Street, and I was just robbed. I came home from work, and my front door was open. I went inside, and no one was there. They have gone through all of my stuff. My TV is missing; my laptop is missing, and probably a lot of other items that I'm unsure of."

This is translated as, "City Units, contact on a Burg Report 1234 Orange Street."

Many people do not know the difference between robbery, burglary, and theft.

I have to go off on a slight tangent here. Stick with me.

Theft is when someone takes something from someone or a business without force. For example, taking a candy bar from a grocery store. If force is used or implied, then it becomes a robbery. An example would be a finger gun inside a coat pocket asking a teller at a bank to give them all their money. Finally, when someone breaks into a secured area, like a fenced-in yard with a gate or a home, to take items, it's considered a burglary.

Marilyn Johnson was burglarized.

The significance of the word *report* in the transmission implies it is not in progress and a routine response to the scene is acceptable. If Ms. Johnson got home and the subjects were inside, this call would be a Burg in Progress. It changes the response. I would send all available units in progress. They would respond to the scene with lights and sirens. The transmissions would get a little longer, with many descriptions of what Ms. Johnson is seeing.

Thank you for sticking with me on that one. It's not essential that you, as a citizen, know the difference between theft, robbery, and burglary, but now you can impress your dispatcher the next time you're robbed at knifepoint.

Good luck!

"Ma'am, I'm trying to explain to you," Jon says to his newest victim.

I twisted in my chair to hear better.

"Ok, it is raining quite hard right now. Are you experiencing an emergency there?" Jon asked.

"Yes! I almost ran off the roadway," a female RP said hysterically.

"Ok, but did you run off the roadway?" Jon asked.

"No."

"Alright, so you are still driving, right?"

"Yes."

"So, is the roadway being washed away?" Jon asked.

I was impressed Jon had lasted so long with an aggressive caller. Usually, he's popping off at this point.

Maybe management had talked to him again recently? He usually calms down after a reprimand.

"No, there's just a lot of water on the roads. I almost got run off the roadway!" she screamed.

"Ok, I do still not understand the emergency."

"I ALMOST ran off the roadway!"

"Ok, so do you need an ambulance, fire truck, or a police officer to talk to you?" Jon asked. He was still trying to figure out what she thought law enforcement could do about water in the roadway.

"No," she said.

"Right, well, it is raining quite hard right now, so everyone should be driving carefully or not at all if you can avoid it. Law enforcement cannot do anything about the rain," Jon explained while remaining calm. I wondered what had happened to the Jon, whom I knew and loved.

"Well, someone might get hurt!" she exclaimed.

"Ok, when they do, call me right back, and we'll do something about it then. Thanks."

There he is.

Someone might get hurt under most circumstances. People call about deer or other wild animals all the time as well. I certainly understand if they impede traffic or if someone just hit one. However, I'll never understand when someone calls in a deer, coyote, or raccoon just to report their sightings to law enforcement. The animals are simply outside; that is where they live.

August 12ᵀᴴ, 2017 – 12 Hour Shift

It's mind-blowing how many people call 911 when they see someone in their neighborhood they do not recognize. Folks who are just walking innocently on the street. Their minds travel to strange places.

"He could be a murderer."

"He is clearly prowling vehicles,"

Or my absolute favorite, "I just get a bad feeling about this."

Unfortunately, we dispatch these types of calls, and 99% of the time, it's an average person walking on the sidewalk. That 1% when someone commits a crime makes us liable. Which is why we have to check.

Unlike the 2002 blockbuster hit 'Minority Report' starring Tom Cruise, we do not have a future crimes division. As a result, we can't do anything with could-be or might-be crimes. Instead, many of our callers will try to get a response based on potential problems.

"I can't handle people today," Terrance said as he joined Jon, Laura, and me.

"Oh no, what's going on?" Laura asked.

It's not often that Terrance complains. On the contrary, he's usually one of our cooler heads in the dispatch center.

"I got a call from this woman who claimed a guy was breaking into a car. I started getting the normal information, location, yadda, yadda. I asked about the vehicle he was breaking into. She said she did not know. I was like ok, so how do you know that he's breaking into a vehicle if you can't see a vehicle? She changes her story, saying he *might* break into a vehicle," Terrance paused.

"Let me guess, walking while black?" I asked.[5]

"Possibly. I never got that far. I asked for more details about what she saw. She said she did not know the person, and he was walking near the vehicles on the public street. I asked about tools, but nothing. I asked about weapons, but none. She couldn't give me a single specific detail. Finally, I asked if she wanted to speak to an officer about it. Of course, she said no. So I thanked her for the info and hung up the phone." Terrance exhaled loudly. "I normally have more patience than this, but today these people are getting on my nerves."

"Yeah, usually you're cool as a cucumber," Laura said.

"We all have our off days. Shake it off, Tiger. You got this!" I said.

"Oh, it doesn't stop there. There's more," Terrance said.

"Sorry, continue."

"You know how people will try to dispatch on *potential crimes* to get someone else in trouble or exaggerate the situation to make the cops drive faster?" Terrence asked.

We nodded.

"I somehow had both in a single call. First, a dude says there is domestic violence at an address. Then, he's being evasive with the questioning. Finally, he admits to me that it is

---

[5] Happens so often, we have a term for it. Check your privilege people.

his ex-wife's house. He's reporting domestic violence in progress, and of course, the new boyfriend has a gun."

"Of course," I said.

"The caller tells me to expedite the response because the new boyfriend might kill her. To which I asked, what makes you think they will kill someone? He says because he has a gun. I explain that many folks have guns and don't kill people. Then I followed up with did someone say they were going to kill someone? No."

"Was he even calling from the location? Like outside her house or anything?" Laura asked.

"Nope," Terrance said. "Basically, he's upset and trying to get the new boyfriend in trouble and inconvenience the ex-wife. But, since it is *possible* that this was happening, I have to put in a call anyway."

"Yep," Laura said.

"Oh yeah, that was my call," Jon said. "She was pissed that he called 911. Apparently, they are fighting over the custody of their children, and he's not winning."

"Sounds like it's for the best, especially if that's his maturity level," Laura said.

At 911, we need the facts of the situation as it currently exists. If someone might kill someone because they said, "I am going to kill my boyfriend," there becomes a reason to send the police. It's a fact that they said these words, and there's reason for concern.

Just about every situation has the potential to go in just about any direction. Speculating to a 911 dispatcher gets you nowhere.

We have heard it all.

We are also usually tired of it all.

When you call 911, give the facts. Provide specifics of a crime. Don't make things up. We'll know.

15
In Conclusion

Dispatch: 911, Where is your emergency?

Female Caller: Yes, I'd like to report a crime.

Dispatch: Ok, what would you like to report?

Female Caller: I had a roommate that moved out, and he stole my car.

Dispatch: Ok, do you know where he may have taken it?

Female Caller: Well, it's back.

Dispatch: He brought the car back?

Female Caller: Yes!

Dispatch: Uhm, then how do you know it was taken?

Female Caller: Well, he fixed the tires, took it somewhere to do that, and then brought it back.

Dispatch: So, let me clarify this to ensure I am hearing it correctly. You want to report that your ex-roommate took your vehicle without permission and returned it in better condition than he took it in?

Female Caller: Yes!!

I love my job. I can't imagine doing anything different. Every day is something new. No two days are ever alike, and just when I think I have heard it all, I get a curve ball thrown at me. I started *From The 911 Files* as an occasional Facebook post to share some of the funny things I encounter with my friends and family. I have a taste for the weird, sadistic, and sometimes dark humor. Perhaps some of my friends and family might enjoy these stories as well. It evolved from there, and I was encouraged to write this book. It has taken me years to figure out how to put this together, and I hope you've enjoyed reading it as much as I have enjoyed living through these stories.

Not everyone can do this job. It takes a strong-willed, fast-thinker, fast-talker, fast-typist with dragon-thick skin. We are yelled at, cursed at, and absolutely belittled by people. All this while still performing at peak levels. Otherwise, the outcome could quite literally be death. Any action or inaction on my part could result in someone's life. That weight constantly put on someone's shoulders is a lot. Especially when you cannot physically be there to do anything. We have to perform 100% audibly.

In my agency, to be hired, an applicant must apply, go through a background investigation, take a pre-employment stress test, interview with the operations manager, take a psychological evaluation, consultation with a psychologist, take a polygraph with a detective, take a drug test, take a hearing test, and pass a final interview with the director. It can take several months before you're offered a position. After that, you have up to two years to complete the training program. Employees are still considered novice level until they have completed about five years of full-time dispatching.

We do have great benefits but only average wages. People do not do this for the money. This is a labor of love. We work 24 hours a day, on holidays, weekends, birthdays, and anniversaries, and must miss out a lot in our social lives.

Enjoyment of what we do is the only explanation I can provide. I could make more money elsewhere. In fact, I took a massive pay cut when I started this line of work. I could get a job with better hours, have weekends off, and see my friends more often, but I choose to stay.

First responders are just a different breed of people. It is in our blood. We get to see the most horrific side of humanity several hundred times a day. We talk to people in their darkest hours, repeatedly. Sometimes, we are the last voice a person hears in their life. We must sit here helplessly and listen as someone else's life changes forever. Then we must brush it off and move on to the next call, frequently with no break in between.

How do we do it?

With an irrefutable sense of humor!

We are a sick, twisted bunch of individuals with an even darker sense of humor. When faced with something horrible, you have two options: cry or laugh. It is much easier to find humor than to carry the weight of misery all the time.

At my dispatch center, we kept a blooper reel. Whenever someone had a funny radio transmission, usually a tongue-tied incident, we would save the recording and add it to our archive. One of my favorites came from a former co-worker who thought she would be fired. We had wireless radio microphones, and the batteries would need replacement every few hours. If you were quick enough, you could get the old battery out and the new battery in before the connection was lost in the base. She really struggled to get this done quickly, as most of us did. It took a lot of practice to master.

One day, she finally got it! Excited, she proclaimed, "Fuck yes! I got it! I fucking got it! Fuck yes, I did!"

Unfortunately for her, she also hit the transmitter button, and the entire celebration went out over the airwaves. A police officer nearby ran in and let her know she had a hot mic and was transmitting all of her profanity. It was not done in malice, but the incident did need to be documented, and she did have to speak with the director about it.

Years later, it is just a funny story.

One of my former supervisors had been a dispatcher for over 25 years. She had started with the state patrol and then worked her way up to county and eventually the supervisor role. She was sweet, innocent, and demure, probably in her mid-to-late 60's. She was involved in an e-mail chain with the sheriff and one of the fire chiefs at that time. Both were old-timers and members of the "good ol' boys" club. At one point, the sheriff poked fun at the Fire Chief and commented, "You all just sit around the firehouse all day polishing your knobs." My sweet, ignorant supervisor apparently took this literally.

A few weeks later, a fire engine was heading to the scene of a commercial fire alarm. Halfway there, they were stood down because the alarm company called back to advise it was a false alarm.

The firefighter commented over the radio, "Confirm that we can stand down then?"

"That's affirmative," she said.

"Alright, we'll head back to the station," the firefighter said.

"Well, now you have plenty of time to polish your knobs!" my supervisor said. She was upbeat.

The communication center went silent. I had a grin from ear to ear on my face. No one could believe that she had just said that over the radio. She looked around and saw that everyone was staring at her in disbelief.

"What?" she asked the room.

"Why would you say that on the radio?" asked the other supervisor.

"What? We were just being catty. It's not completely unprofessional," she said.

"I don't think you know what you just said."

The supervisor leaned in and whispered the explanation of the sexual innuendo she had broadcasted. Her face went from her usual pale to a bright red. She was mortified. She had to unplug and hide in the office for a few hours. I would not let her live that down for many years to follow, and since I am bringing it up again here, it is forever immortalized.[1]

One death per shift has been my average for years. Sometimes it is suicide. Sometimes a murder. Sometimes it's a child, an adult, or an elderly individual by natural causes. But if every death affected me, I would be unable to do my job. It's important to separate myself from the incident. If I am taking a 911 call and the caller is in crisis, I remind myself they are in crisis, not me. The incident is not happening directly to me,

---

[1] God, I hope she reads this.

and it's my job to remain calm so I can effectively help the person calling.

The only calls that make me spin out and forget my training are kid calls. It might be because I am a parent that I can empathize the most with these types of RPs. I am the most affected when bad things happen to kids and babies. I consciously take a fraction of a second to breathe and remind myself of my training. Then, I get right back into the call and do my job. After disconnecting, I find myself looking to fill the void left by the call. If no other calls are coming in, I need to do something to keep my brain busy. Otherwise, I will feel myself spiraling. This is the closest thing I can relate to a panic attack.

Despite my best efforts, I am only human.

The precipice of being able to find humor in horrible situations started with my mother. When I was young, my grandmother was diagnosed with Alzheimer's disease. She was relatively young at 53 years old and went downhill quickly. I have zero memories of my grandmother before the illness.

With my father working full time, my mother was a stay-at-home mom, and she took on the caretaker role for my grandmother. Watching a loved family member fall ill with a disease is miserable. Alzheimer's slowly attacks your brain, and you start to forget things; appointments, where items are placed, etc. Then, eventually, you begin to forget family members and lose control over motor functions.

My grandma eventually reverted into a child-like state, which was fun for me since we were mentally the same age. My mother would joke about having three babies in diapers: my brother, grandmother, and me. Grandma would forget where she was, who she was, and who we were. Devastated, my mother chose to find the humor in the situation rather than feel the constant burden and sadness. The disease was going to take my grandmother, that part was clear. How we choose to react to the situations dealt with is what defines us as people.

My grandmother died in 1994. I have few memories of her; unfortunately, all are after the disease. I could focus on how I never got to know my real grandmother. Only the grandmother after the disease. However, I chose to remember the fun times and how my mother handled the whole situation through laughter.

Laughter and finding the humor in life can heal or at least lessen the sting of many bad situations. One time, my best friend and I took a road trip to Portland, Oregon. We had a great trip, and on the way back, somewhere in central Wyoming, a semi-truck exiting the freeway hit us. Thankfully, neither of us was injured, my vehicle was pretty banged up, and I even got a ticket because I did not have valid proof of insurance (I forgot to replace the old card with the new one). I only remember taking silly pictures to recreate the event from that day. Nevertheless, we had a great story to share, and I still remember the entire trip as one of my favorite road trips I have ever taken in my life.

Life is a balancing act, we have the light with the dark, the good with the bad, and the funny with the sad. We have many choices to make in life, and sometimes things just happen to us. Even when we feel like choice has been taken from us, we still have the option of how to react.

I choose to laugh; I encourage you to do the same.

Life may be scary, so remember, none of us are getting out alive. Be kind to each other.

Acknowledgments

I would like to express my deep gratitude to Miranda, whose invaluable contributions were instrumental in bringing this book to life. Miranda's tireless efforts, a keen eye for detail, and unwavering dedication to excellence have been an inspiration throughout the writing process.

From the earliest drafts to the final edits, Miranda's feedback and insights have been essential in shaping this story into the best possible version of itself. Her commitment to the project and willingness to go above and beyond the call of duty have made her indispensable.

I am also grateful for Miranda's friendship and support. Her positivity, sense of humor, and unwavering belief in the power of storytelling were a constant source of encouragement throughout this journey.

To Miranda, thank you for your hard work, creativity, and unwavering commitment to excellence. This book would not have been possible without you, and I am grateful for everything you have done to help bring it to fruition.

About The Author

Jackson Anhalt is a rising star in the world of non-fiction writing, known for his gripping stories and page-turning suspense. His latest work, "From the 911 Files," is a departure from his usual genre, a heartwarming and uplifting story following a group of dispatchers in a 911 call center in their day-to-day ups and downs of life.

Anhalt's writing is characterized by his deep understanding of the human condition and ability to create relatable and memorable characters. His storytelling is infused with humor, empathy, and a sense of optimism that inspires and uplifts readers.

Anhalt has always had a passion for storytelling. He began his writing career as a freelance journalist, covering local events and human interest stories before turning his attention to non-fiction writing and blogging.

"From the 911 Files" is a testament to Anhalt's versatility as a writer and his ability to tackle a wide range of subjects with sensitivity and skill. Despite its departure from his usual genre, the book has been well-received by readers and critics alike, who have praised its warmth, humor, and heart.

With "From the 911 Files," Jackson Anhalt cements his place as a writer to watch, a talent whose boundless creativity and skillful storytelling will continue to captivate readers for years to come.

Made in United States
Troutdale, OR
11/20/2024

25094434R00184